Discussing Abortion

Volume 367

Independence Educational Publishers

First published by Independence Educational Publishers

The Studio, High Green

Great Shelford

Cambridge CB22 5EG

England

© Independence 2020

Copyright

Photocopy licence

ISBN-13: 978 1 86168 824 8

Printed in Great Britain

Zenith Print Group

Contents

Introduction

Discussing Abortion is Volume 367 in the **ISSUES** series. The aim of the series is to offer current, diverse information about important issues in our world, from a UK perspective.

ABOUT DISCUSSING ABORTION

Globally, one in four pregnancies ends in abortion. This highly emotive and contentious topic is rarely out of the news. This book looks at abortion legislation around the world, the changes that have been made and the impact these changes have on women's health. It also explores the opposing views of the pro-choice and pro-life lobbies.

OUR SOURCES

Titles in the **ISSUES** series are designed to function as educational resource books, providing a balanced overview of a specific subject.

The information in our books is comprised of facts, articles and opinions from many different sources, including:

◆ Newspaper reports and opinion pieces

◆ Website factsheets

◆ Magazine and journal articles

◆ Statistics and surveys

◆ Government reports

◆ Literature from special interest groups.

A NOTE ON CRITICAL EVALUATION

Because the information reprinted here is from a number of different sources, readers should bear in mind the origin of the text and whether the source is likely to have a particular bias when presenting information (or when conducting their research). It is hoped that, as you read about the many aspects of the issues explored in this book, you will critically evaluate the information presented.

It is important that you decide whether you are being presented with facts or opinions. Does the writer give a biased or unbiased report? If an opinion is being expressed, do you agree with the writer? Is there potential bias to the 'facts' or statistics behind an article?

ASSIGNMENTS

In the back of this book, you will find a selection of assignments designed to help you engage with the articles you have been reading and to explore your own opinions. Some tasks will take longer than others and there is a mixture of design, writing and research-based activities that you can complete alone or in a group.

FURTHER RESEARCH

At the end of each article we have listed its source and a website that you can visit if you would like to conduct your own research. Please remember to critically evaluate any sources that you consult and consider whether the information you are viewing is accurate and unbiased.

Useful Websites

www.abortionrightscampaign.ie

www.bpas.org

www.catholicherald.co.uk

www.downtoearth.org.in

www.fpa.org.uk

www.gov.uk

www.humanism.org.uk

wtwww.independent.co.uk

www.inews.co.uk

www.news-decoder.com

www.nhs.uk

www.politicshome.com

www.righttolife.org.uk

www.telegraph.co.uk

www.theconversation.com

www.theguardian.com

www.who.int.news-room/fact-sheets

Overview – Abortion

An abortion is the medical process of ending a pregnancy so it doesn't result in the birth of a baby.

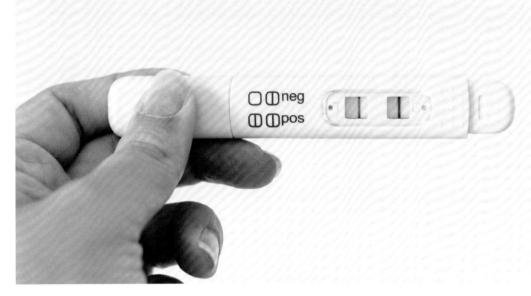

- It's also sometimes known as a termination.

- The pregnancy is ended either by taking medications or having a minor surgical procedure.

- One in three women will have an abortion in their lifetime.

How to get an abortion

Abortions can only be carried out in an NHS hospital or a licensed clinic, and are usually available free of charge on the NHS.

There are three main ways to get an abortion on the NHS:

- contact an abortion provider directly – the British Pregnancy Advisory Service (BPAS), Marie Stopes UK and the National Unplanned Pregnancy Advisory Service (NUPAS) can tell you about eligibility and services in your area

- speak to your GP and ask for a referral to an abortion service – your GP should refer you to another doctor if he or she has any objections to abortion

- visit a contraception clinic, family planning clinic, sexual health clinic or genitourinary medicine (GUM) clinic and ask for a referral to an abortion service.

The pregnancy is ended either by taking medications or having a minor surgical procedure.

One in three women will have an abortion in their lifetime.

When an abortion can be carried out

Most abortions in England, Wales and Scotland are carried out before 24 weeks of pregnancy.

They can be carried out after 24 weeks in certain circumstances – for example, if the mother's life is at risk or the child would be born with a severe disability.

The length of your pregnancy is calculated from the first day of your last period. If you're not sure how long you've been pregnant, you may need an ultrasound scan to check.

Abortions are simpler and safer the earlier they're carried out. Getting advice early on will give you more time to make a decision if you're unsure.

Deciding to have an abortion

Some women may be certain they want to have an abortion, while others may find it more difficult to make a decision.

The decision to have an abortion is yours alone. But all women requesting an abortion should be offered the opportunity to discuss their options and choices with, and receive support from, a trained pregnancy counsellor.

Impartial information and support is available from:

- your GP or another doctor at your GP practice
- a counselling service at the abortion clinic
- organisations such as the FPA, Brook (for under-25s), BPAS, Marie Stopes UK and NUPAS – but beware of so-called 'crisis pregnancy centres' that claim to provide impartial advice but often do not.

You may also want to speak to your partner, friends or family, but you don't need to discuss it with anyone else and they don't have a say in the final decision.

If you don't want to tell anyone, your details will be kept confidential. If you're under 16, your parents don't usually need to be told. Information about an abortion doesn't go on your medical record.

What happens during an abortion

Before having an abortion, you'll attend an appointment to talk about your decision and what happens next.

Whenever possible, you should be given a choice of how you would like the abortion to be carried out.

There are two options:

- medical abortion (the 'abortion pill') – you take two medications, usually 24 to 48 hours apart, to induce a miscarriage
- surgical abortion – you have a minor procedure to remove the pregnancy and normally go home soon afterwards.

After an abortion, you'll probably need to take things easy for a few days. It's likely you'll experience some discomfort and vaginal bleeding for up to two weeks.

Risks of an abortion

Abortions are safest if they're carried out as early as possible in pregnancy.

Most women won't experience any problems, but there is a small risk of complications, such as:

- infection of the womb – occurs in up to 1 in every 10 abortions
- some of the pregnancy remaining in the womb – occurs in up to 1 in every 20 abortions
- excessive bleeding – occurs in about 1 in every 1,000 abortions
- damage to the entrance of the womb (cervix) – occurs in up to 1 in every 100 surgical abortions
- damage to the womb – occurs in 1 in every 250 to 1,000 surgical abortions and less than 1 in 1,000 medical abortions carried out at 12 to 24 weeks.

If complications do occur, further treatment – including surgery – may be required.

Having an abortion won't affect your chances of becoming pregnant again and having normal pregnancies in the future.

In fact, you may be able to get pregnant immediately afterwards and should use contraception if you want to avoid this.

August 2019

Abortion law

England, Scotland and Wales.

In 1967, Parliament passed the Abortion Act, later amended by the Human Fertilisation and Embryology Act 1990.

It applies to England, Wales and Scotland. It does not extend to Northern Ireland.

Rather than making abortion legal, the Act makes exceptions to the 1861 Offences Against the Person Act which made abortion an offence punishable by life in prison.

Under the 1967 Act, a doctor can legally perform an abortion, which has been authorised by two doctors, up to 23 weeks and 6 days of pregnancy if continuing the pregnancy would involve risk, greater than if the pregnancy was terminated, of injury to the physical or mental health of the pregnant woman or any existing children of her family.

An abortion can be authorised and carried out with no time limit if:

◆ the termination is necessary to prevent grave permanent injury to the physical or mental health of the pregnant woman

◆ there is a risk to the life of the pregnant woman, greater than if the pregnancy were terminated

◆ there is substantial risk that if the child were born it would suffer from such physical or mental abnormalities as to be seriously handicapped.

Availability

Until recently, all abortions in England, Scotland and Wales were required to take place in an NHS hospital or a place approved by the Secretary of State, for example, a registered clinic.

Wales and Scotland have recently updated their laws on early medical abortion, with women now able to take the second stage of the medication at home. The UK Government has said that home use in England will be legalised by the end of 2018.

Conscientious objection

Health professionals are not required to perform or participate in an abortion if they have a moral or conscientious objection. They still have a duty to participate in an abortion, if it is necessary to save the life of a woman or to prevent serious injury.

Northern Ireland

In Northern Ireland, outdated laws force women to continue with pregnancy against their will.

The Abortion Act 1967 which covers England, Scotland and Wales, was never extended to Northern Ireland.

Reproductive rights in Northern Ireland are covered by sections 58 and 59 of the Offences Against the Person Act 1861 and section 25 of the Criminal Justice Act (Northern Ireland) 1945.

Section 5 of the Criminal Law Act (Northern Ireland) 1967, created the offence of withholding information if a person knows or believes an offence has been committed. This places healthcare professionals at risk of prosecution if they fail to disclose knowledge of an illegal abortion, and deters women from seeking medical support.

Many women from Northern Ireland are forced to travel to other parts of the UK to have abortions. In 2016/17, only 13 abortions were performed in Northern Irish hospitals. This compares to at least 861 women and girls from Northern Ireland who travelled to England and Wales for an abortion in 2017.

Given the large numbers of women travelling from Northern Ireland, the UK Government's 2017 announcement that Northern Irish women would be eligible for free NHS abortions in England was welcome.

However, it is not a substitute for a comprehensive reform of the law. It also excludes many people who are unable or unwilling to travel. This includes victims of domestic violence, refugees without confirmed immigration status who are unable to travel, those who are too young to travel alone and those with complex health needs.

19 September 2018

www.fpa.org.uk

Abortion statistics, England and Wales: 2018

An extract from summary information from the abortion notification forms returned to the Chief Medical Officers of England and Wales.

Key points in 2018

Total abortions have increased for residents of England & Wales.	There were 200,608 abortions for women resident in England and Wales in 2018 and 205,295 abortions including non-residents. The figure for women resident in England and Wales is an increase of 4% since 2017 and the highest number recorded.
17.4 per 1,000¹ resident women had an abortion.	Abortion rate increased from 16.7 per 1,000 women in 2017. The rate has decreased from 2008, when 17.5 per 1,000 of resident women had an abortion.
Abortions for non-residents of England & Wales increased slightly from 2017.	4,687 abortions for non-residents were carried out in England and Wales, slightly above the number carried out in 2017 (4,633). The 2018 total is a decrease of 32% since 2008. 61% of non-residents travel from the Republic of Ireland and 22% from Northern Ireland.
Over the last 10 years abortion rates have decreased year on year for women aged under 18. Abortion rates have been increasing for women aged over 35.	The under 18 crude abortion rate for 2018 is 8.1 per 1,000 resident women. This is less than half the 2008 rate of 18.9 per 1,000. The abortion rate for women aged 35 or over is 9.2 per 1,000 resident women in 2018. This increased from a rate of 6.7 per 1,000 women in 2008.
Almost all abortions in England & Wales were funded by the NHS in 2018, with most of these abortions taking place in the independent sector.	98% of abortions were funded by the NHS, the same level since 2013, but an increase from 91% in 2008. 72% of abortions took place in the independent sector, an increase of 2 percentage points from 2017 and an increase of 19 percentage points from 2008.
3,269 abortions were due to the risk that the child would be born seriously handicapped².	This figure has remained constant since 2008. Four out of every five abortions were carried out under 10 weeks gestation in 2018.
71% of abortions were medically induced.	This is higher than in 2017 (66%), and almost double the proportion in 2008 (37%).
39% of women who had an abortion had one or more previous abortions.	This is an increase of 1 percentage point since 2017 (38%), and an increase of 6 percentage points since 2008.

1 Based on Age Standardised Rate (ASR). All age standardised rates presented in this publication are based on the 2013 ESP. See Annex A for the 2013 ESP and how the rate is derived.
2 Under "ground E" of the Abortion Act. See main publication for details of methodology and data quality.

Overall number and rate of abortions

In total, there were 205,295 abortions notified as taking place in England and Wales in 2018, of which 200,608 were to residents of England and Wales. This represents an age-standardised abortion rate of 17.4 per 1,000 resident women aged 15–44[3]. The 2018 rate has increased since 2017 (16.7 per 1,000 resident women aged 15–44) but is lower than the peak in 2007 of 17.9 abortions per 1,000 resident women.

Figure 1: Age standardised abortion rate per 1,000 women aged 15-44, England and Wales, 1970 to 2018

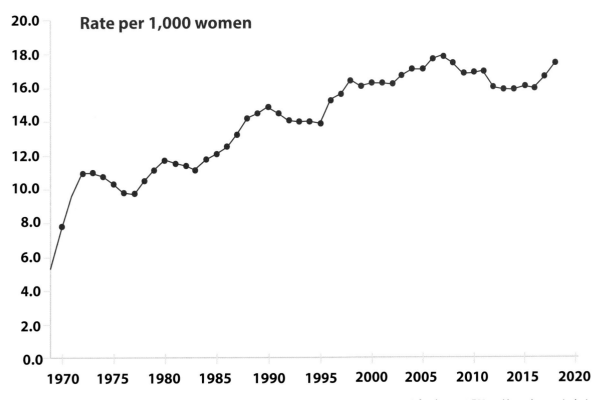

All age standardised rates presented in this publication are based on the 2013 ESP. See Annex A for the 2013 ESP and how the rate is derived.

Age

The abortion rate in 2018 was highest for women at the age of 21 (at 30.7 per 1,000 women). Last year the highest rate was for women aged 20 (29.1 per 1,000 women).

There were 1,267 abortions to girls aged under 16 (0.6% of the total). Of these, 363 were to girls aged under 15 (0.2% of the total). There were also 746 to women aged 45 or over (0.4%). (Table 4a).

Abortion rate per 1,000 women by single year of age, England and Wales, 2008 and 2018

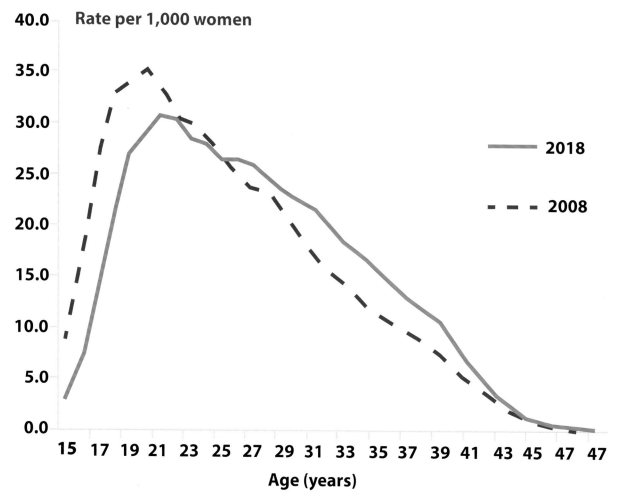

Abortion rates for those aged under 18 have declined over the last ten years. The decline is particularly marked in the under-16 age group where the rates are less than a third of what they were in 2008. The abortion rate in the 16–17 age group has more than halved from a peak of 22.2 per 1,000 women in 2008, to 10.0 per 1,000 women in 2018.

The abortion rate for 18–19-year olds also declined from 33.3 per 1,000 women in 2008 to 23.8 per 1,000 women in 2018, and for those aged 20–24 the rate declined from 31.6 per 1,000 women in 2008 to 29.2 per 1,000 women in 2018, though there has been a slight increase for those aged 20–24 from 28.2 per 1,000 women in 2017.

For women aged 25–29, the rate of abortion per 1,000 women was 25.3 in 2018. This is an increase from 23.9 in 2008. Rates for this age group have increased in recent years, from their lowest level in 2012 of 21.8 abortions per 1,000 women.

The rates for women aged 30–34 have increased from 15.6 per 1,000 women in 2008 to 19.9 in 2018, and rates for women aged 35 and over have also increased from 6.7 per 1,000 women in 2008 to 9.2 per 1,000 women in 2018.

13 June 2019

A Humanist discussion on abortion

Humanists seek to live good lives without religious or superstitious beliefs. They use reason, experience and respect for others when thinking about moral issues, not obedience to dogmatic rules. So in thinking about abortion a humanist would consider the evidence, the probable consequences, and the rights and wishes of everyone involved, trying to find the kindest course of action or the one that would do the least harm.

Abortion is an issue that demonstrates the difficulties of rigid rules in moral decision making. Medical science has advanced to the point where we have options that were unthinkable even a few generations ago and where old rules cannot cope with new facts.

Some medical facts

◆ Some very premature babies can now be kept alive, which has altered ideas about when foetuses become human beings with human rights. The law in England and Wales is based on the fact that after 24 weeks the foetus is often viable, in that with medical assistance it can survive outside the womb.

◆ Many illnesses and disabilities can now be diagnosed long before birth.

◆ Some very ill or disabled babies who would probably once have died before or shortly after birth can now be kept alive.

◆ The sex of a foetus can be known well before birth (and some parents would like to be able to choose the sex of their child).

◆ Genetic research makes it increasingly likely that parents will be able to know, or even to choose, other characteristics for their unborn child. A few will want to reject some foetuses.

◆ Abortions can be performed safely, though they can occasionally cause medical or psychological problems.

These are in themselves morally neutral medical facts, but they bring with them the necessity to make moral choices and to consider who should make those choices. Doctors? Politicians? Religious leaders? Medical ethics committees? Individual women? Their partners?

Some views on abortion

Some examples of contemporary rules and views about abortion will perhaps demonstrate the complexity of the problem.

Some religious people think that all human life is sacred, that life begins at conception, and so abortion is always wrong (and some also believe that contraception is wrong, which leads to even more unwanted pregnancies). But a humanist would argue that the idea of 'sacredness' is unhelpful if one has to choose between risking the life of the mother or the life of the unborn foetus. (This is very rare these days, and the choice is most often about the quality of life of either the mother or the foetus or both.)

People often argue that it is not for doctors 'to play God'and that it is for God to decide matters of life and death. But it could be said that all medical interventions are 'playing God' (even your childhood vaccinations may have kept you alive longer than 'God' planned) so we have to decide for ourselves how we use medical powers. Arguments which invoke God are unconvincing to those who do not believe in gods, and laws should not be based on claims which rely on religious faith.

Some (non-religious) moral philosophers have argued that full consciousness begins only after birth or even later, and so foetuses and infants are not full human beings with human rights.

Doctors have a range of opinions on abortion, but tend to give the medical interests of the mother (which may include her mental health) the most weight when making decisions.

Some doctors and nurses dislike carrying out abortions because they feel that their job is to save life, not to destroy it.

Some people believe that a woman has absolute rights over her own body which override those of any unborn foetus. You might like to read Judith Jarvis Thomson's *A Defense of Abortion* which states a feminist case for abortion very clearly.

The law in England, Scotland and Wales permits abortion before the 24th week of pregnancy if two doctors agree that there is a risk to the life or the mental or physical health of the mother if the pregnancy continues, or there will be a risk to the mental or physical health of other children in the family. However, there is no time limit if there is a substantial risk that the baby will be born severely disabled, or there is a grave risk of death or permanent injury (mental or physical) to the mother. In effect this means that almost every woman who wants an abortion and is persistent in seeking one before the 24th week can obtain one. However, some women who do not realise that they are pregnant until too late (perhaps because they are very young or because they are menopausal) may not be able to have abortions though they would have qualified on other grounds.

The humanist view

The current law is permissive: it does not impose abortion on anyone who does not want one or does not want to perform one. So even within the law, individuals have to make moral choices. How do humanists pick their way between these conflicting ideas? There is not one, correct humanist view on abortion. However humanists tend to converge on liberal, 'pro-choice' stance. Humanists value happiness and personal choice, and many actively campaigned for legalised abortion in the 1960s. Although humanists do not think all life is 'sacred' they do respect life, and much in this debate hinges on when one thinks human life begins. Humanists tend to think that – on the basis of scientific evidence about foetal development – a foetus does not become a person, with its own feelings and rights, until well after conception.

Because humanists take happiness and suffering as foremost moral considerations, quality of life will often trump the preservation of life at all costs, if the two come into conflict. (Assisted dying is another example.) The probable quality of life of the baby, the woman, rights and wishes of the father and the rest of the family, and the doctors and nurses involved, would all have to be given due weight. There is plenty of room for debate about how much weight each individual should have, but most humanists put the interests of the woman first, since she would have to complete the pregnancy and probably care for the baby, whose happiness would largely depend on hers. She also exists already with other responsibilities and rights and feelings that can be taken into account – unlike those of the unborn foetus which cannot be so surely ascertained.

Of course, all possible options should be explored and decisions should be informed ones. Adoption of the unwanted baby might be the best solution in some cases, or on reflection a woman might decide that she could look after a sick or disabled child. Or she might decide that she cannot offer this child a life worth living and abortion is the better choice. She will need to consider the long-term effects as well as the immediate ones. It is unlikely to be an easy decision, and requiring an abortion is a situation that most women would prefer to avoid.

For society as a whole, as well as for the children themselves, it is better if every child is a wanted child. However, abortion is not the best way of avoiding unwanted children, and improved sex education, easily available contraception, and better education and opportunities for young women, can all help to reduce the number of abortions. But as long as abortion is needed as a last resort, most humanists would agree that society should provide safe legal facilities. The alternatives, which would inevitably include illegal abortions, are far worse.

Questions to think about and discuss

◆ Is abortion in the case of conception after rape more justified than other abortions?

◆ Would a humanist favour abortion if a woman wanted one because her pregnancy was interfering with her holiday plans? Why (not)?

◆ Why do humanists think contraception is better than abortion?

◆ Are there any good arguments against adoption of unwanted babies?

◆ Should doctors and nurses impose their moral views on patients? Yes? Sometimes? Never?

◆ Should religious people impose their views on abortion on non-religious people? Yes? Sometimes? Never?

◆ Should parents be able to choose the sex of their child? Should they be able to abort a foetus of the 'wrong' sex?

◆ At what point does a foetus become a human being? Does this affect the humanist view of abortion? Does this affect your view of abortion?

◆ Can infanticide ever be right?

◆ Should abortion ever be carried out on a non-consenting woman, e.g. one too young to give legal consent or one in a coma?

◆ How are you deciding your answers to these questions? What principles and arguments influence your answers?

◆ How is the humanist view on this issue similar to that of other worldviews you have come across? How is it different?

The above information is reprinted with kind permission from Humanists UK.
© Humanists UK 2020

www.humanism.org.uk

2020 begins with record-breaking attendances at pro-life marches

Thousands of pro-life campaigners marched in Denver and Chicago on Saturday calling for an end to abortion.

The marches are part of a nationwide effort to draw attention to the more than 600,000 abortion procedures carried out in the US each year and call for laws that support women and protect unborn babies.

These two marches took place just two weeks before the national March for Life in Washington, which attracted hundreds of thousands of pro-life marchers last year.

A record-breaking 9,000 people attended the March for Life in Chicago, Illinois which had the theme 'Life Empowers: Pro-Life is Pro-Woman!'

Ahead of the march, the March for Life Chicago board president, Dawn Fitzpatrick, told the *Chicago Tribune*, "There's more people in Illinois and the Midwest who recognize the urgency of this. We recognise that there's a human being that's created from the moment of conception."

Over 8,000 people gathered for the Celebrate Life rally in Denver, Colorado carrying signs that read, 'Civil rights begin in the womb' and 'I am the pro-life generation.'

Participants were given the chance to sign a petition to support a policy on the 2020 Colorado ballot, which seeks to protect unborn babies by ending the practise of late-term abortion in the state.

Under Initiative 120, a person conducting an abortion after 22 weeks of pregnancy could be subject to having their medical licence suspended for at least three years, except in cases where the life of the mother is at risk.

According to the Charlotte Lozier Institute, a pro-life research group, in 2018, there were 323 abortions that occurred in Colorado at 21 weeks or later in a pregnancy. The survival rate for babies born at 22 weeks has doubled over the past decade prompting new guidance in the UK, allowing doctors to try to save babies born as early as 22 weeks into a pregnancy.

Colorado became the first state to allow abortion in limited instances in 1967. Currently, the state doesn't have any restrictions on when a pregnancy can be terminated and abortion rights advocates have pushed to keep it that way. Abortion providers in the state can opt-out of providing post-abortion care and don't require parental consent for minors seeking abortions.

Among the speakers at the rally was Archbishop Samuel J. Aquila, who shared how his experience of working in a hospital as a college student and seeing aborted babies there changed his life.

Revealing details about an abortion procedure that still impacts him decades later, Aquila told Colorado Public Radio: "It is tragic and I remember being stunned… I can still remember the horror on the young woman's face [during the abortion]."

Referring to Initiative 120, the Catholic archbishop assured attendees of the rally that it does not amount to an endorsement of abortion during the earlier stages of a pregnancy.

"But we also desire to protect, even in increments, the gift of given life. We are not voting for abortion, nor are we saying we agree with abortion up to 22 weeks. What we are

saying, is that we respect life, and we respect it for all the pregnancy," Aquila said.

David Bereit, co-founder of pro-life group 40 Days For Life, said: "We are not going to rest because what started in Colorado will end in Colorado... Colorado has tried other ballot initiatives on the pro-life side in the past that have failed. This is the one that a large majority of people agree upon."

Pro-life demonstrations across the world have also seen record numbers in attendance in recent years. In 2019, over 50,000 Slovakians called on the country's leaders to protect unborn babies. Pro-life demonstrations in Northern Ireland reached over 20,000 people, over 11,000 marched for life in the Netherlands, over 5,000 people marched for life in the UK, and over 2,000 people attended New Zealand's March for Life.

A spokesperson for Right To Life UK, Catherine Robinson said:

"What a wonderful way to begin 2020, continuing with the trend of the record-breaking numbers of people attending pro-life demonstrations that we have seen over the past few years, not just overseas but also in the UK.

"In 2020 and beyond, we will be using this momentum and the momentum of a more pro-life parliament to call on the Government to urgently bring forward increased support for women with unplanned pregnancies to reduce the tragic number of abortions that happen each year.

"We are excited to see the pro-life movement continue to grow around the world this year and are hopeful of innovative new laws and safeguards that will support women and protect unborn babies."

13 January 2020

Diana Johnson: Let's end the Victorian stigma and create a 21st century abortion law

Whether they are in Belfast, Bangor or Bath, women deserve modern, humane and properly regulated access to abortion.

Diana Johnson MP

Abortion is governed by the oldest legal framework of any healthcare treatment in our country. Our current abortion laws date back to the Offences Against the Person Act 1861, which states that any woman who procures her own miscarriage and anyone who assists her can go to prison for life.

The 1967 Abortion Act gave a route for women in England and Wales to have an abortion, setting out specific exemptions and conditions when abortion would be legal.

These included the need for signatures from two doctors agreeing, for example, that termination is necessary to prevent permanent injury to the physical or mental health of the pregnant woman.

However, this 1967 Act never applied to Northern Ireland. This means that a woman in Northern Ireland seeking an abortion after being impregnated through rape or incest could face a heavier criminal punishment than the perpetrator – the real criminal.

However, even in England or Wales, a woman who buys abortion tablets online is still committing a criminal offence punishable by life imprisonment. It's often the most vulnerable women, finding it difficult to access termination services, who turn to the internet.

Women on Web, a doctor-led online medical service, say that 16% of women cite domestic or 'honour' violence, and 8% intimate partner violence, as reasons to seek tablets online. Women impregnated by rape are often denied contraception – sometimes forcibly – to keep them bound to the abuser.

Whether it's in Belfast, Bangor or Bath, women need a modern, supportive, humane, properly regulated medical regime that encourages them to come forward for the best professional advice and treatment – not drive them, isolated and scared, into the unregulated internet pills market.

This June, the Supreme Court found that Northern Ireland's current abortion laws breach women's human rights.

With the Northern Ireland Assembly not sitting since January 2017, UK politicians can no longer look away while vulnerable women in Northern Ireland, often suffering in desperate circumstances, have their human rights breached.

Polling research released on 10 October 2018 by Amnesty International shows that 65% of people in Northern Ireland believe that 'having an abortion should not be a crime'; and 66% supported the view that in the absence of devolved government 'Westminster should legislate to reform the law'.

That's why my Abortion Bill, supported by MPs from five Westminster parties, top professional medical bodies and human rights groups, seeks to decriminalise abortion across England, Wales and Northern Ireland.

My Bill ensures that up to 24 weeks foetal gestation women and clinicians would no longer be subject to the criminal law. However, decriminalisation wouldn't mean the deregulation of abortion. My aim is more effective regulation – fit for purpose in the 21st century internet age.

The existing body of law and professional standards governing medical procedures would stay to ensure safe termination services. It would remain a crime to offer abortion services without being registered to do so, while anyone supplying the medication needed for a medical abortion without a legal prescription would breach the Human Medicines Regulations 2012.

My Bill will also strengthen protection for women. Anyone – an abusive partner, for example – who ends a pregnancy against a woman's wishes through violence, or by administering abortion pills without the woman's knowledge, would be subject to a life sentence. My Bill also protects doctors and nurses who conscientiously object to abortion – extending this right to Northern Ireland.

It's time to take the Victorian misogynist stigma out of our abortion laws and to have laws that are woman-centred – removing criminal courts from decisions that a woman takes about her own body.

22 October 2018

www.politicshome.com

10 reasons to decriminalise abortion

1 It's out of date

The 1861 Offences Against the Person Act (OAPA), which criminalises abortion, is a Victorian piece of legislation that fossilises values well out of step with those cherished in Britain today.

2 It's patronising to women

Under the 1967 Abortion Act, which provided exemptions from prosecution under the OAPA but did not decriminalise abortion, a woman cannot decide for herself to have an abortion.

This decision has to be made on her behalf, by two doctors. This paternalistic approach sits at odds with every other clinical procedure. In the 21st century, a woman who ends her own pregnancy without the permission of 2 doctors can be 'kept in penal servitude for life'.

3 It discriminates against women

The criminalisation of abortion makes a mockery of the equal status that is accorded to women in any other area of life, and represents discrimination against women.

Without the ability to control their fertility, women would have not achieved the level of educational and workplace equality that younger generations can rightly take for granted. Abortion cannot solve all the problems of sexual equality; but without the ability to exercise reproductive choice, women have no hope of planning their own life course.

It is entirely inappropriate that a procedure which has underpinned such enormous and beneficial social change should sit within criminal law.

4 It is at odds with fundamental legal principles

The fact that abortion remains within criminal law sits at odds with other legal principles of bodily autonomy. A pregnant woman cannot be compelled to undergo any intervention against her wishes, even if her foetus may die as a result. A mother cannot be forced to donate a kidney to a dying child, but she can be compelled to sustain a foetus against her will.

5. The punishment is entirely disproportionate

A young woman who takes abortion pills bought online could be sent to prison for 12 years. A doctor who provides safe abortion care to a woman who requests it without the approval of his or her colleague could be sent to prison for 12 years. If we do not believe these people should be imprisoned we should not accept a law which stipulates that they should.

6. Public opinion has changed since the 1960s

The 1967 Act was also developed in a context where public opinion was far more ambivalent about abortion than it is today. Two-thirds of people today say that abortion should be allowed according to a woman's choice, compared to 37% in 1983.

7. Abortion in Britain today is a fact of life

There are around 200,000 abortions a year. One in three women will have an abortion in their lifetime. Sexual health policy supports the provision of abortion, and 98% of abortions are funded by the NHS.

It is bizarre that it should be governed by criminal law rather than regulated in the same way as any other healthcare procedure.

8. It prevents best clinical practice

The fact that unlike any other medical procedure and for no clinical reason whatsoever two doctors must authorise every request for an abortion inevitably causes needless delays. Women undergoing miscarriage treatment are able to take the pills they need to pass an early pregnancy in the comfort of their own home.

The law prevents women undergoing early abortion from doing this. Abortion procedures today are safe and straightforward, and do not need to be performed by doctors. However, the law currently denies nurses and midwives a larger role in the provision of care.

9. It puts doctors off caring for women

One of the aims of the Abortion Act was to protect doctors from prosecution when performing legal abortions. But misinterpretations of the law leave doctors exposed to the 'chilling effect' of smear campaigns and challenges by opponents of abortion. This impacts seriously upon women's care, with doctors more reluctant to provide it over fears of prosecution.

10. Removing it from the criminal law will not increase abortions

One of the aims of the Abortion Act was to protect doctors from prosecution when performing legal abortions. But misinterpretations of the law leave doctors exposed to the 'chilling effect' of smear campaigns and challenges by opponents of abortion. This impacts seriously upon women's care, with doctors more reluctant to provide it over fears of prosecution.

Why abortion is more than a political debate

Abortion is wrapped up in politics in many nations including the US. But one in four pregnancies ends in abortion, making it a global health issue.

By Maggie Fox

Abortion is one of the most common medical procedures globally.

It is grist for a raging political debate in the United States, nearly half a century after the highest court in the country ruled that women have the right to choose whether or not to end a pregnancy.

But abortion is far more than a political issue framed in ethical, religious or moral terms. It is also a matter of public health, for society and individual women.

The Guttmacher Institute, set up to study reproductive health, estimates that a quarter of all pregnancies globally are ended by abortion.

Abortion is constantly in the news, and in some countries it causes more political debates than any other single issue.

In the United States, abortion rights are being attacked by the administration of President Donald Trump and in conservative-led states such as Alabama and Georgia. Ireland, meanwhile, shocked the world and many of its own residents when voters chose to repeal one of the world's most restrictive bans on abortion in 2018.

Abortion bans across much of Africa are being challenged in courts, even as religious campaigners use social media and billboards to depict abortion as a sin.

Religious opposition

Yet in many countries, abortion is not a political issue. It's freely available to women in 67 countries, with another 56 countries allowing it on health grounds. Abortion is banned outright in 26 countries, according to the Center for Reproductive Rights. Other countries limit elective abortion to earlier stages of gestation.

Most opposition to abortion rights stems from religious beliefs. The Roman Catholic Church, for instance, teaches that abortion is a sin because it ends a human life.

'Human life must be respected and protected absolutely from the moment of conception. From the first moment of his existence, a human being must be recognized as having the rights of a person – among which is the inviolable right of every innocent being to life,' the Vatican says in the *Catechism of the Catholic Church*.

This was not always the case.

In centuries past, the Vatican defined pregnancy and human life as beginning when the foetus 'quickened', or started to move around in a way that the mother could feel. The same went for non-Catholic countries, including Britain and its colonies, until the 1800s. It wasn't until modern medicine pinpointed the moment of egg meeting sperm that the idea of life at conception became common.

Healthcare need

But doctors around the world, and large majorities of voters in countries where abortion is legal, see embryos and foetuses as part of the woman's body, not separate persons, at least until some stage in the pregnancy. And to them, abortion is above all a medical procedure.

'Safe, legal abortion is a necessary component of women's health care,' the American College of Obstetricians and Gynecologists (ACOG), which represents women's health specialists, says in its position statement. 'Access to safe pregnancy termination options remains of vital importance.'

'It is a basic healthcare need for millions of women, girls and others who can become pregnant,' the human rights group Amnesty International says.

Women can need abortions for a variety of reasons, ACOG says. 'They include, but are not limited to, contraceptive failure, barriers to contraceptive use and access, rape, incest, intimate partner violence, foetal anomalies, and exposure to teratogenic medications,' it says. Teratogenic medications are drugs that can severely damage a developing foetus.

Other reasons include heart and kidney conditions, life-threatening high blood pressure and the rupture of the placenta – the organ that links a woman and the fetus. These conditions may be 'so severe that an abortion is the only measure to preserve a woman's health or save her life,' ACOG says.

Sometimes abortions are performed because the fetus has abnormalities. These can range from genetic conditions to hydrocephalus, a condition that can leave a developing foetus without any normal brain tissue. Such abnormalities might not be diagnosed until late in a pregnancy.

Abortion as political tool

Abortions can be done surgically, using a variety of methods, or medically, using drugs to stop the pregnancy and induce labour to expel the foetus or embryo.

When done by medical professionals in a clean setting and using the correct equipment, the World Health Organization and ACOG say the procedure is safer than pregnancy. Women are more likely to suffer complications or die during childbirth than they are during or after an abortion.

The earlier an abortion is done, the safer it is.

Dr Jen Gunter, an obstetrician who has worked in both Canada and the United States, said she has had to perform very late-term abortions for medical reasons when a woman knew her baby would die at or soon after birth but decided to take it to term, anyway.

'The pregnant person thought they could make it to their due date, but they just can't take it anymore. Or maybe their blood pressure is sneaking up and the idea of risking their life for a non-viable pregnancy is not what they want or their doctors recommend,' Gunter wrote on her blog.

Amnesty, the World Health Organization, ACOG, the American Medical Association and many other groups say laws that limit or outlaw abortion hurt women and do little to stop abortion from happening.

'Let's be clear, if you are truly 'pro-life' you'd agree with these procedures because they save women. Not in an abstract way, but sometimes it is in a 'this-infection-is-killing-you-and-we-need-to-help-you-right-now' kind of way,' Gunter wrote.

'The one thing I've learned from my experience is that efforts to stop abortion after 20 weeks are nothing about life or compassion or good medicine. It is simply wielding the misery of women (and those who love them) as a political tool.'

Challenging Roe v. Wade

In 1973, an important US Supreme Court decision called Roe v. Wade established a woman's right to abortion, based on her right to privacy. Amnesty International agrees that the matter is personal.

"Human rights law clearly spells out that decisions about your body are yours alone – this is what is known as bodily autonomy," the group said. "Forcing someone to carry on an unwanted pregnancy, or forcing them to seek out an unsafe abortion, is a violation of their human rights, including the rights to privacy and bodily autonomy."

But conservatives across the United States are challenging this concept. US states where abortion opponents dominate legislatures and governor's offices have passed a variety of laws designed to challenge Roe v. Wade.

They include laws limiting how late in pregnancy an abortion may be performed; laws that establish strict medical requirements for abortion clinics that make it difficult or impossible for them to operate; laws that cut funding for organisations that provide or mention abortion; and laws that require doctors to tell patients that abortion is terminating the life of a human being.

ACOG, Planned Parenthood and other groups say these laws are not based on accurate medical need or practice.

The gag rule

The impact of US policies can extend beyond the United States. Soon after he took office in 2017, Trump re-instituted a policy known as the Mexico City policy. First instituted by former President Ronald Reagan in 1984, it forbids federal funding for organisations providing abortions.

Washington has flip-flopped on this policy ever since. Democratic presidents – Bill Clinton and Barack Obama – have rescinded it. Republicans – George W. Bush and Trump – put it back into place. Trump's administration has taken it further, forbidding US federal funding to any organisation that provides or refers women to abortion service – even if they don't use federal funds for those services.

The policy, also called 'the gag rule,' forces groups to give up all US funding if they want to keep abortion in the mix of services they provide or if they want to support other groups that do.

But research shows the policy does not reduce the number of abortions and even makes them more common because people find it harder to get contraceptive care and counselling.

In a study published in June, Nina Brooks and colleagues from Stanford University in California found a 40% increase in abortions among women in 26 African countries in years when the gag rule was in place, compared to years when it was not.

They compared abortion rates globally during the Clinton, Bush and Obama administrations. 'Our findings suggest how a US policy that aims to restrict federal funding for abortion services can lead unintentionally to more – and

probably riskier – abortions in poor countries,' they wrote in a report published in *The Lancet* medical journal.

This is in no small part because the United States is the biggest source of aid for medical and health services. When US aid money disappears, organisations struggle to provide even basic health care, including birth control but also other health services such as HIV/AIDS prevention and primary care services.

Unsafe abortions

Women do not stop seeking abortions just because they are difficult or illegal to get, the international group Medecins Sans Frontières/Doctors Without Borders, says. "When a woman or girl is determined to end her pregnancy she will do so, regardless of the safety and legality of the procedure," the group said.

"The history of unsafe abortion is marked by dangerous methods – including the use of sharp sticks inserted through the vagina and cervix into the uterus; ingestion of toxic substances such as bleach; herbal preparations inserted into the vagina; infliction of trauma, such as hitting the abdomen or falling." Most methods don't end the pregnancy, but injure or kill the woman.

The WHO studied abortions around the world between 2010 and 2014. 'Around 25 million unsafe abortions were estimated to have taken place worldwide each year, almost all in developing countries,' the WHO concluded.

3 July 2019

Preventing unsafe abortion

KEY FACTS

- Between 2010–2014, on average, 56 million induced (safe and unsafe) abortions occurred worldwide each year.

- There were 35 induced abortions per 1,000 women aged between 15–44 years.

- 25% of all pregnancies ended in an induced abortion.

- The rate of abortions was higher in developing regions than in developed regions.

- Around 25 million unsafe abortions were estimated to have taken place worldwide each year, almost all in developing countries (1).

- Among these, 8 million were carried out in the least-safe or dangerous conditions.

- Over half of all estimated unsafe abortions globally were in Asia.

- 3 out of 4 abortions that occurred in Africa and Latin America were unsafe.

- The risk of dying from an unsafe abortion was the highest in Africa.

- Each year between 4.7%–13.2% of maternal deaths can be attributed to unsafe abortion (2).

- Around 7 million women are admitted to hospitals every year in developing countries, as a result of unsafe abortion (3).

- The annual cost of treating major complications from unsafe abortion is estimated at US$553 million (4).

- Safe abortion must be provided or supported by a trained person using WHO-recommended methods appropriate for the pregnancy duration.

- Almost every abortion death and disability could be prevented through sexuality education, use of effective contraception, provision of safe, legal induced abortion, and timely care for complications (5).

Abortions are safe if they are done with a method recommended by WHO that is appropriate to the pregnancy duration and if the person providing or supporting the abortion is trained. Such abortions can be done using tablets (medical abortion) or a simple outpatient procedure.

Unsafe abortion occurs when a pregnancy is terminated either by persons lacking the necessary skills or in an environment that does not conform to minimal medical standards, or both. The people, skills and medical standards considered safe in the provision of induced abortions are different for medical abortion (which is performed with drugs alone), and surgical abortion (which is performed with a manual or electric aspirator). Skills and medical standards required for safe abortion also vary depending upon the duration of the pregnancy and evolving scientific advances.

◆ They are less safe, when done using outdated methods like sharp curettage even if the provider is trained or if women using tablets do not have access to proper information or to a trained person if they need help.

◆ Abortions are dangerous or least safe when they involve ingestion of caustic substances or untrained persons use dangerous methods such as insertion of foreign bodies, or use of traditional concoctions.

Women, including adolescents, with unwanted pregnancies often resort to unsafe abortion when they cannot access safe abortion. Barriers to accessing safe abortion include:

◆ restrictive laws

◆ poor availability of services

◆ high cost

◆ stigma

◆ conscientious objection of healthcare providers and

◆ unnecessary requirements, such as mandatory waiting periods, mandatory counselling, provision of misleading information, third-party authorization, and medically unnecessary tests that delay care.

Scope of the problem

Based on data from 2010–2014 there are approximately 25 million unsafe abortions annually. Of these one-third or approximately 8 million were performed under the least safe conditions by untrained persons using dangerous and invasive methods. Unsafe abortions lead to an estimated 7 million complications (3).

In developed regions, it is estimated that 30 women die for every 100,000 unsafe abortions. That number rises to 220 deaths per 100,000 unsafe abortions in developing regions and 520 deaths per 100,000 unsafe abortions in sub-Saharan Africa.

Mortality from unsafe abortion disproportionately affects women in Africa. While the continent accounts for 29% of all unsafe abortions, it sees 62% of unsafe abortion-related deaths (1).

Who is at risk?

Any woman with an unwanted pregnancy who cannot access safe abortion is at risk of unsafe abortion. Women living in low-income countries and poor women are more likely to have an unsafe abortion. Deaths and injuries are higher when unsafe abortion is performed later in pregnancy. The rate of unsafe abortions is higher where access to effective contraception and safe abortion is limited or unavailable.

Complications of unsafe abortion requiring emergency care

Following unsafe abortion, women may experience a range of harms that affect their quality of life and well-being, with some women experiencing life-threatening complications. The major life-threatening complications resulting from the least safe abortions are haemorrhage, infection, and injury to the genital tract and internal organs. Unsafe abortions when performed under least-safe conditions can lead to complications such as:

◆ incomplete abortion (failure to remove or expel all of the pregnancy tissue from the uterus)

◆ haemorrhage (heavy bleeding)

◆ infection

◆ uterine perforation (caused when the uterus is pierced by a sharp object)

◆ damage to the genital tract and internal organs by inserting dangerous objects such as sticks, knitting needles, or broken glass into the vagina or anus.

Signs and symptoms

An accurate initial assessment is essential to ensure appropriate treatment and prompt referral for complications of unsafe abortion. The critical signs and symptoms of complications that require immediate attention include:

◆ abnormal vaginal bleeding

◆ abdominal pain

◆ infection

◆ shock (collapse of the circulatory system).

Complications of unsafe abortion can be difficult to diagnose. For example, a woman with an extra-uterine or ectopic pregnancy (abnormal development of a fertilised egg outside of the uterus) may

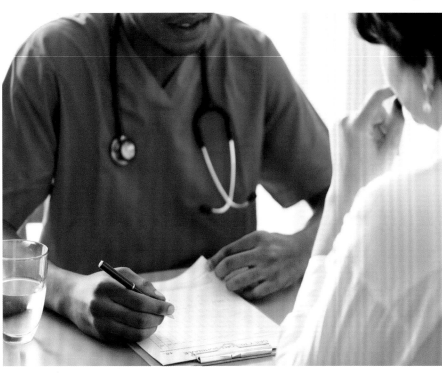

have symptoms similar to those of incomplete abortion. It is essential, therefore, for healthcare personnel to be prepared to make referrals and arrange transport to a facility where a definitive diagnosis can be made and appropriate care can be delivered quickly.

Treatment and care

Complications arising from unsafe abortions and their treatments include:

- Haemorrhage: timely treatment of heavy blood loss is critical, as delays can be fatal.

- Infection: treatment with antibiotics along with evacuation of any remaining pregnancy tissue from the uterus as soon as possible.

- Injury to the genital tract and/or internal organs: if this is suspected, early referral to an appropriate level of health care is essential.

Access to treatment for abortion complications

Healthcare providers are obligated to provide life-saving medical care to any woman who suffers abortion-related complications, including treatment of complications from unsafe abortion, regardless of the legal grounds for abortion. However, in some cases, treatment of abortion complications is administered only on the condition that the woman provides information about the person(s) who performed the illegal abortion.

The practice of extracting confessions from women seeking emergency medical care as a result of illegal abortion puts women's lives at risk. The legal requirement for doctors and other healthcare personnel to report cases of women who have undergone abortion, delays care and increases the risks to women's health and lives. UN human rights standards call on countries to provide immediate and unconditional treatment to anyone seeking emergency medical care (6).

Prevention and control

Unsafe abortion can be prevented through:

- comprehensive sexuality education;

- prevention of unintended pregnancy through use of effective contraception, including emergency contraception; and

- provision of safe, legal abortion.

In addition, deaths and disability from unsafe abortion can be reduced through the timely provision of emergency treatment of complications (5).

Economic impact

In addition to the deaths and disabilities caused by unsafe abortion, there are major social and financial costs to women, families, communities and health systems. In 2006, it was estimated that US$553 million was spent treating serious consequences of unsafe abortion (4). An additional US$375 million would be required to fully meet the unmet need for treatment of complications from unsafe abortion (4).

WHO response
Evidence-based resources

WHO provides global technical and policy guidance on the use of contraception to prevent unintended pregnancy, safe abortion and treatment of complications from unsafe abortion. In 2012, WHO published updated technical and policy guidance on safe abortion.

An interactive online database containing comprehensive information on the abortion laws, policies, health standards and guidelines for all countries is available at http://www.srhr.org/abortion-policies.

Technical support to countries

Upon request, WHO provides technical support to countries to adapt sexual and reproductive health guidelines to specific contexts and strengthen national policies and programmes related to contraception and safe abortion care.

Research

WHO is a cosponsor of the UNDP/UNFPA/UNICEF/WHO/World Bank Special Programme of Research, Development and Research Training in Human Reproduction, which carries out research on clinical care as well as implementation research on community and health systems approaches to preventing unsafe abortion. It also monitors the global burden of unsafe abortion and its consequences.

26 June 2019

(1) Ganatra B, Gerdts C, Rossier C, Johnson Jr B R, Tuncalp Ö, Assifi A, Sedgh G, Singh S, Bankole A, Popinchalk A, Bearak J, Kang Z, Alkema L. Global, regional, and subregional classification of abortions by safety, 2010–14: estimates from a Bayesian hierarchical model. The Lancet. 2017 Sep

(2) Say L, Chou D, Gemmill A, Tunçalp Ö, Moller AB, Daniels J, Gülmezoglu AM, Temmerman M, Alkema L. Global causes of maternal death: a WHO systematic analysis. Lancet Glob Health. 2014 Jun; 2(6):e323-33.

(3) Singh S, Maddow-Zimet I. Facility-based treatment for medical complications resulting from unsafe pregnancy termination in the developing world, 2012: a review of evidence from 26 countries. BJOG 2015; published online Aug 19. DOI:10.1111/1471-0528.13552.

(4) Vlassoff et al. Economic impact of unsafe abortion-related morbidity and mortality: evidence and estimation challenges. Brighton, Institute of Development Studies, 2008 (IDS Research Reports 59).

(5) Haddad L. Unsafe Abortion: Unnecessary Maternal Mortality. Rev Obstet Gynecol. 2009 Spring; 2(2): 122–126.

(6) Human Rights Committee; Committee Against Torture; Committee on the Elimination of Discrimination Against Women.

www.who.int.news-room/fact-sheets

A Global Issue

Abortion law in Ireland

As of 1 January 2019, the law allowing access to abortion in the Republic of Ireland is the Health (Regulation of Termination of Pregnancy) Act 2018. This legislation followed from the 66.4% Yes vote in the referendum to repeal the Eighth Amendment in May 2018.

The Act is the first to make abortion on request legal in Ireland, however it is far from perfect. Here, we outline some of the key problems we want our TDs and Senators to resolve when the Act comes up for review.

Problem 1: Time limits and a mandatory waiting period will mean some people will still be forced to travel or import abortion pills illegally

The Act legalises abortion on request up to 12 weeks of pregnancy, subject to a requirement to wait three days between seeing your doctor and receiving the abortion. The way the Act defines it, 12 weeks of pregnancy is around ten weeks since conception. Some people could be close to this time limit or beyond it when they find out they are pregnant, such as teenagers or women who have irregular menstrual cycles. Combined with the mandatory three-day wait, the timeframe for access to abortion will be too narrow for many people. There is no evidence that waiting periods are medically necessary or have any impact on a pregnant person's decision. In fact, evidence consistently finds that waiting periods only create practical and psychological hardship for pregnant people.

These barriers will force some people to travel abroad for care, or force them to order safe but illegal pills online. It will be as if the Eighth had never been repealed.

Problem 2: Refusal of care on grounds of conscience creates barriers for pregnant people

Evidence from other countries has shown that refusal to provide care, or so-called 'conscientious objection,' is a major barrier to abortion access. The Act permits medical practitioners to refuse to care for patients on grounds of conscience except in emergency situations. In countries like Italy, refusal to provide abortion care has become widespread, due in large part to 'convenient objectors' who claim conscientious objection but are often simply unwilling to provide this service for other reasons. The result

is that although abortion in Italy is technically legal, it can be practically impossible to access, particularly in rural or isolated areas.

Pregnant people should receive the best standard of care when they need abortion and not be passed around from one doctor or hospital to the next. The Government should look to Sweden and Finland, where the patients' rights come first and refusals on grounds of conscience are not permitted.

Problem 3: The Act endangers the health of pregnant people

The Act is supposed to allow abortion where a woman's health is a stake, but ambiguous wording is used in this section. We are troubled by the phrase '[risk] of serious harm to health'. There is no medical definition of 'serious harm' and in the face of unclear regulations, pregnant people who are unwell may be wrongly denied care and the threat to their health could worsen. We have already seen this problem in Ireland. In 2017, the Abortion Support Network reported that two women who had attempted suicide more than once were denied abortions, even though there was a threat to their lives. ASN's founder Mara Clarke said, 'Both of these women were basically told that they weren't suicidal enough.'

Numerous medical experts testified before the Joint Oireachtas Committee that health risks can escalate quickly and doctors need to use their clinical judgment and expertise to care for their patients. Ambiguous terms in law are bound to cause confusion, and pregnant people will suffer the consequences.

Problem 4: A doctor, friend or family member could still face a 14-year prison sentence for helping someone access abortion

The Irish people voted for abortion to be a healthcare issue not a criminal act – but the Act still criminalises anyone who assists a pregnant person to obtain an abortion outside of the provisions of the Act, with a prison sentence of up to 14 years. This is at odds with the spirit of repealing the Eighth and contradicts medical best practice, which advocates for the full decriminalisation of abortion. Criminalisation could impact a parent or partner who orders abortion pills, such as happened to a teenager's mother who has been charged in an ongoing case in Northern Ireland. The likely result will be medical professionals interpreting the law very conservatively, and patients being denied care.

Problem 5: The Act uses exclusively gendered language

The Act uses the word 'woman' throughout to refer to any person who needs or wants an abortion. This is not compatible with the Gender Recognition Act 2015, and excludes transgender and non-binary people, who can and do become pregnant and avail of abortion. While women and girls are the largest groups affected by restricted access to abortion, the law should not discriminate or leave anyone behind. This problem can be easily fixed by replacing the word 'woman' with 'person' or 'person who is pregnant' throughout the Act.

It's time to speak up

Our reproductive rights are now in the hands of our elected representatives. To fix the problems set out above, we all need to contact our TDs consistently and tell them we need the best possible abortion legislation. The improvement of the Health Act needs to be a key issue in any upcoming General Elections. Please call, write to or meet with your TD today to ask them to support amendments to improve this Act when it comes up for review.

15 January 2019

Northern Ireland has been forced to change its abortion law – here's how it happened.

An article from The Conversation.

By Jennifer Thomson

THE CONVERSATION

Of all the strange twists and turns that UK politics have taken in recent years, the sudden legalisation of abortion and same-sex marriage in Northern Ireland is perhaps one of the most unexpected. At a time when the Northern Irish Democratic Unionist Party still props up the Westminster Government, change seemed unlikely. The party is staunchly socially conservative and largely opposed to reform on both issues. Yet thanks to movement from Westminster, abortion has now been decriminalised in Northern Ireland.

Until 21 October 2019, abortion was only legal in Northern Ireland if there was a severe and long-term physical or mental risk to the woman's health. The Abortion Act introduced in

the rest of the UK in 1967 was never extended to Northern Ireland, which has meant that every year hundreds of women have had to travel to England for terminations. They even had to pay for them until Westminster changed the law in 2018 to cover the cost.

Recent rulings in the High Court in Belfast and the Supreme Court in London have stated that the situation in Northern Ireland was incompatible with human rights legislation.

Changes from Westminster

In January 2017, the devolved government of Northern Ireland broke down over a dispute about a renewable heating initiative and was suspended. In July 2019, Westminster passed legislation which said that if the Northern Irish Assembly had not been re-established by 21 October then the law in Northern Ireland would be changed.

That means that a new legal framework for abortion law must be in place by 31 March 2020 and same-sex marriage and opposite-sex civil partnerships must be introduced by 13 January 2020.

A consultation will shortly be opened to debate what the law should ultimately look like. However, we already know that, from 2020, abortions will be permitted in a much wider range of cases than the very restricted legal situation in Northern Ireland has previously allowed. The UK Government now has a legal duty to introduce access to abortion in Northern Ireland by the 2020 March deadline along the lines of the 2018 UN Committee on the *Elimination of Discrimination Against Women* report. This will allow for abortion at the very least in cases of rape, incest, severe foetal abnormality and threats to a woman's physical or mental health.

In the meantime, interim arrangements have been put in place so that abortion is now decriminalised. GPs will be encouraged to put women seeking terminations in contact with a central booking system which can arrange NHS-funded treatment in England.

Nudged by Westminster

Despite these monumental developments, it's not guaranteed that Northern Ireland will end up with the same abortion laws as the rest of the UK. There may still be an uphill battle to implement a similarly liberal framework.

Indeed, these legislative changes have not been driven by the government in Northern Ireland, but from Westminster. The changes do reflect a growing cross-party consensus in Westminster that Northern Ireland should not continue to be allowed to impose different rules on its citizens than other parts of the UK. The motion that prompted the change in Northern Ireland passed overwhelmingly by 332 to 99 votes in the House of Commons.

The changes at Westminster around abortion and same-sex marriage were pushed by backbenchers – Labour MP Stella Creasy (who was also behind the 2018 change to funding for women travelling from Northern Ireland) and Connor McGinn (the Northern Irish-born Labour MP for St Helens North). Their distance from the front benches may have been helpful in terms of the partisan support that these successful motions enjoyed.

Yet key Conservative women were also vocally supportive of the changes, including Penny Mordaunt, the then women and equalities minister, who declared that the situation for Northern Irish women was 'appalling'.

The DUP has opposed the changes but has been treading a careful line. To block Westminster, it would have to get the Northern Ireland Assembly up and running again, which would have involved political compromises on other issues that it is not yet ready to make.

But senior DUP members, including party leader Arlene Foster have been present at sizeable anti-abortion rallies outside Stormont, home to the assembly.

The DUP attended the assembly just as the deadline on the legislation approached in what was supposed to be an attempt to get the Northern Ireland Government up and running again. But Sinn Fein chose not to take part and the event ended up being largely symbolic. It was over within in an hour and descended into farce, with various parties walking out en masse.

Yet the DUP's position against liberalising abortion may suggest there will be difficulties ahead in cementing substantial change by the end of March next year. Resistant voices may have influence during the consultation. As a result, at least in the interim, we will still see significant numbers of women having to travel to England for treatment.

Abortion equality across the four regions of the UK is yet to be fully guaranteed.

22 October 2019

Poland has some of the strictest abortion laws. This German NGO has a solution

Group members offer up their couches, help with translating and accompany the women to hospital.

By Dylan Brethour

Across the globe, the rise of right-wing parties has stirred up the fight over abortion. In Poland, which has some of the most restrictive laws in Europe, women can only get an abortion in cases of rape or incest, when the pregnancy poses a serious threat to a woman's health, or when there is a severe foetal abnormality.

In cases when it is allowed, doctors often refuse to perform the procedure.

In 2016, thousands took part in the so-called Black Protests across the country when the ruling Law and Justice party proposed a total ban on the procedure. The Government backed down but abortion remains illegal in most circumstances and the current parliament is making moves to restrict access even further.

Enter the Berlin-based activist group Ciocia Basia. Their mission? To help women in Poland access abortions – in Germany.

The clue to what makes Ciocia Basia unique is in the name, which means 'Aunt Basia' in Polish. The suggestion of a warm, supportive and trustworthy older relative is no accident.

The group provides psychological as well as financial assistance, with members offering up their couches, translating and accompanying the women to hospital.

Ann and Aleksandra are two of the roughly 20-strong group of regular volunteers. They asked only their first names be used.

"Having to get this procedure abroad is stressful, so we're there to comfort them and help make sure everything is organised so they don't have to do anything other than to come here and have the procedure," Ann tells *The Independent*.

The women find Ciocia Basia online or through word of mouth, and demand for their help is growing.

"According to the latest governmental report, we had about 1,000 legal abortions in 2018," says Krystyna Kacpura, executive director of the Federation for Women and Family Planning NGO in Poland.

"We have five million women of reproductive age, limited access to contraception – especially emergency contraception – and no sexual education.

"Can you imagine 1,000 abortions in a country with five million women? No."

Kacpura estimates that roughly 150,000 Polish women have abortions each year, using pills, illegal private clinics or going abroad.

"We call this abortion migration or abortion tourism," she adds.

No one knows how many women harm themselves trying to induce abortions, but Kacpura says doctors working in clinics close to the Polish border tell them they have many cases of unfinished self-performed abortions.

She adds that the restrictive laws have had a disproportionate effect on poorer women who can't pay for travel.

In Ciocia Basia, Aleksandra estimates that at least half of the women wouldn't be able to afford the procedure without their help. But telling the full story of the victims of Poland's abortion law is a challenge.

While there has been pushback from pro-choice protesters, social pressure creates an environment where women are often too frightened and ashamed to speak about their experience of abortion – even anonymously.

"Sometimes we ask for a couple of sentences for other women, and it's impossible because she just wants to forget," Kacpura says.

Women who come to Ciocia Basia feel the weight of that pressure. They always want to explain their decision, even though the volunteers never ask.

Aleksandra says that the reasons they give are incredibly varied, whether "financial, being too young, being too old, having a horrible relationship".

> ## "Trauma is the main framing within the Polish discourse about abortion."
>
> – Aleksandra, Ciocia Basia

About 50 per cent of the women arrive on their own, and often haven't told their family or partner.

"I translate for them at the clinic and usually there's a general feeling of shame and secrecy," she says. "They're usually tense in the beginning but after they see it's treated like a normal medical procedure and everyone is treating them kindly, they relax."

Making abortion seem shadowy and disreputable is seen as one of the most powerful tools of the anti-abortion movement.

Abortion pills such as misoprostol can be discretely provided by pro-choice organisations such as Women on Web – anti-abortion groups may not be able to completely prevent access, but they can weaponise shame to control the discourse surrounding the procedure.

Ann describes one Polish woman's experience of searching for information about abortion: "She was like, 'You have no idea how many names I got called, [people saying] I should die and rot in hell.

Then you find Ciocia Basia and everyone gives you the feeling that you are welcome, that your situation is normal, that you're not a devil just because you want to have a medical procedure.'"

"I think there's a lot of not taking women seriously, not trusting them with their choices," Aleksandra says.

She was raised in Poland and blames the influence of the Catholic church for stigmatising abortion. "This is one of the main topics that they talk about, it's just a huge deal. For some reason, their main ideological goal is to eradicate abortion access completely."

Both she and Ann express frustration at the misinformation surrounding the procedure.

"Trauma is the main framing within the Polish discourse about abortion. Even liberal media perpetuates the myth that it always has to be this traumatic experience, although various studies have shown that the trauma is associated with stigma and not being able to talk to your family," Aleksandra says.

> ## "You have no idea how many names I got called, people saying I should die and rot in hell."
>
> – Anonymous client at Ciocia Basia

"There's a lot of weird dichotomies like 'people who get abortions versus mothers'. People don't realise that's often the same person but at different life stages.

"I often have mothers who already know how much time, stress and emotion it takes to raise a child, and they're like 'I cannot do this again, I already have five kids.'"

Speaking openly about abortion is part of the new wave of activism, as pro-choice groups across the continent come together to defend reproductive rights.

The UK-based Abortion Support Network was the main inspiration for Ciocia Basia. Now, their organisation is part of a larger European network with the same pro-choice goal.

"I wouldn't like a future where groups like ours are necessary," Aleksandra says, "but if it goes the way it's going now, then I hope more will start."

8 September 2019

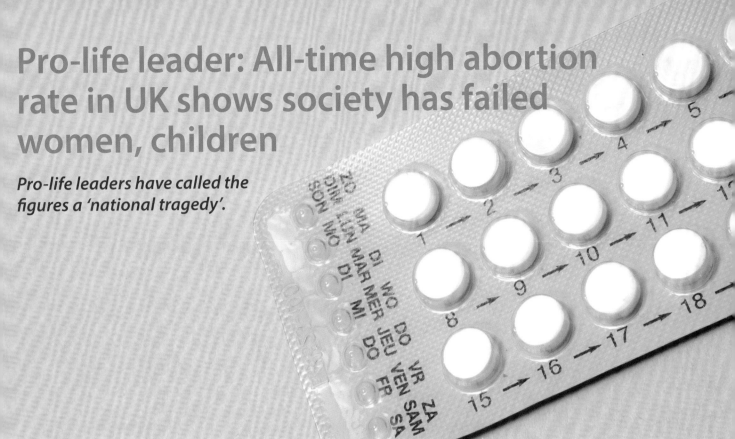

Pro-life leader: All-time high abortion rate in UK shows society has failed women, children

Pro-life leaders have called the figures a 'national tragedy'.

More than 200,000 UK women received an abortion in 2018, setting an all-time high rate of abortion in England and Wales.

The UK Department of Health and Social Services released a study on Wednesday which revealed that last year, 200,608 UK residents and nearly 5,000 more non-residents received an abortion in the UK.

According to the survey, abortions in the country had decreased in 2009, but have steadily increased since 2010. The previous record high was in 2008.

In the last decade, the number of abortions have increased particularly for women who are over 29 and those who already have a family. Over half of the abortions in 2018 were performed on women who have had children or had a still-born birth.

'The rates for women aged 30–34 have increased from 15.6 per 1,000 women in 2008 to 19.9 in 2018, and rates for women aged 35 and over have also increased from 6.7 per 1,000 women in 2008 to 9.2 per 1,000 women in 2018,' the study states.

However, the rate of abortions for women under the age of 18 significantly decreased in the past decade. The 2018 rate reflected a decrease by more than half in the number of teens who received abortions, compared to the rate in 2008.

According to the *Daily Mail,* abortion experts said the trends are complicated. Clare Murphy, director of external affairs for British Pregnancy Advisory Service, said contraception distribution and family planning have both played a part in the numbers.

"Accessible contraceptive services are often focused on the needs of younger women and women over the age of 25 can in particular find themselves excluded from schemes providing free, pharmacy access to emergency contraception," she said.

"However, it is also possible that over the longer term couples are making different decisions about family size and the number of children they can afford and feel able to properly care for."

Following budget cuts to health services, abortion advocates have called for more funding to be provided. Professor Lesley Regan, president of the Royal College of Obstetricians and Gynaecologists, told BBC that the under-funding needs to stop.

"We are calling for an end to fractured commissioning and greater accountability to stop the under-funding and fragmentation of these services which disproportionately affects women," she said.

However, Clare McCarthy, spokesperson for the pro-life non-profit Right to Life, decried the recent record, calling it a 'national tragedy'. According to *The Telegraph,* the pro-life leader said the issue will probably worsen.

"Every one of these abortions represents a failure of our society to protect the lives of babies in the womb and a failure to offer full support to women with unplanned pregnancies," she said.

"Proposals from abortion campaigners to remove legal restrictions around abortion and introduce abortion right to birth would likely see these numbers get even worse."

17 June 2019

Selective abortions kill 22.5 million foetuses in China, India.

Abortions lead to gender ratio distortions in 12 Asian and European countries.

By Kiran Pandey

The natural gender ratio for humans is 100 female babies to 105 male babies. But this ratio has been distorted due to abortions, finds the study conducted across 202 countries. While specifically focusing on how selective abortions by women impact the sex ratio, it focuses on 12 Asian and European countries which favour male babies.

22.5 million females missing in China and India

Nearly 23.1 million females are missing due to sex-selective abortions in 12 Asian and European countries finds the five-year study. The study has revealed the largest differences in gender ratios from China and India. China currently has approximately 11.9 million missing females and India has approximately 10.6 million missing females

China had the worst sex ratio in 2005; less women to produce babies

The sex ratio in China was worst in 2005 where approximately 100 female bables were born in comparison to 118 male births. Even though China lifted a law prohibiting more than one child per couple, population growth has continued to stagnate due to the lack of women to produce babies.

Overall, sex ratio in India has declined from 903 in 2007 to 898 in 2018, as per Niti Aayog.

10 other countries with skewed sex-ratio

The other countries identified with sex ratio imbalance (SRB) were Albania, Armenia, Azerbaijan, Georgia, Hong Kong, Republic of Korea, Montenegro, Taiwan, Tunisia and Vietnam.

What led to sex-selective abortion

Preference for sons and improved technology for prenatal sex diagnosis, along with declining fertility level are the three main factors that led to sex-selective abortion said the study citing a United Nations study. Legal medical abortion for several weeks after onset of pregnancy has also been misused.

Fertility fell to low levels around the world that resulted in a 'squeezing effect'. Sex-selective abortion is a way to avoid large families while still having a male child. Necessary conditions for the occurrence of sex-selective abortions include a large tolerance for induced abortion from both the population and the medical establishment, available techniques for early sex detection, and legal medical abortion for several weeks after onset of pregnancy.

An up-to-date systematic analysis for the SRB – one of the most fundamental demographic indicators – for all countries over time using all available data with reproducible estimation method is urgently needed. So, this global assessment of natural variations in the sex ratio at birth done using a new estimation method must be considered while estimating population in the future for effective policy and programmes, said University of Massachusetts Amherst biostatistician Leontine Alkema, associate professor in the School of Public Health and Health Sciences, who led the study.

17 April 2019

'No girls born' for past three months in area of India covering 132 villages

Any parents found to have carried out female foeticide will face legal action, district magistrate says.

By Chris Baynes

An investigation into suspected sex-selective abortions has been launched by magistrates in a district of northern India after government data showed none of the 216 children born across 132 villages over three months were girls.

Authorities in Uttarkashi, Uttarakhand state, said the official birth rate was 'alarming' and pointed towards widespread female foeticide.

India outlawed the selective abortion of female foetuses in 1994 but the practice remains commonplace in the country, where parents often see boys as breadwinners and girls as costly liabilities.

The last population census, conducted in 2011, found there were only 943 females per 1,000 males in India.

Ashish Chauhan, Uttarkashi's district magistrate, said the area's recent female birth rate – collected by the local health department – was 'suspicious and has highlighted female foeticide'.

The 132 villages where no girls were born over three months have all been marked as part of a "red zone", which means local data will be scrutinised more closely and health workers have been asked to be vigilant.

Any parents found to have carried out female foeticide will face legal action, Mr Chauhan said, in comments reported by the TNN news agency.

Legislative assembly member Gopal Rawat said: "It is shocking to have a zero girl child birth rate in 132 village of the district, as we have rarely heard of seen any incident of female foeticide in the hills.

"I have directed the health department to find out the real cause of such alarming figures and to take serious action to resolve it."

He added authorities would also launch "a massive awareness campaign" in the hope of reversing the trend.

Last year an Indian government report found about 63 million women were statistically 'missing' from the country's population due to a preference for male children.

"Issues relating to son preference are a matter for Indian society as a whole to reflect upon," the report said.

In India's patriarchal society, male children are seen as future breadwinners and caregivers who have an obligation to look after their parents when they age.

Daughters are seen as costly because parents are often pressured to pay dowries when they marry, despite the custom being banned in 1961.

Last year police found 19 aborted female foetuses near a hospital in the state of Maharashtra. They were discovered by officers investigating the death of a woman who had undergone an illegal abortion.

22 July 2019

Here's what legalising abortion has meant for US women

What was it like in the US before abortion was legal? A doctor recalls botched, amateur procedures and fears health risks if abortion is re-criminalised.

By Susan Ruel

A woman's 'right to choose' whether to carry a pregnancy to term has long been a contentious issue in the United States, even though the Supreme Court legalised abortion in its 1973 Roe v. Wade decision.

The landmark ruling put the United States among the 30% of countries worldwide that permit abortion on the basis of the mother's request, according to a United Nations report on world abortion policies.

Recently, the long-smouldering US battle over abortion rights has escalated to levels not seen since Roe was decided. A number of states with legislatures controlled by the conservative Republican Party have passed laws curbing or curtailing access to abortion – even in cases of rape or incest.

By the end of May, more than 350 bills that would restrict abortion had been proposed in state legislatures this year, according to the Guttmacher Institute, a reproductive rights research group.

In May, Alabama lawmakers voted to ban abortions in nearly all cases. Georgia, Kentucky, Louisiana, Missouri, Mississippi and Ohio have approved 'heartbeat bills' that effectively prohibit abortions after six to eight weeks of pregnancy, when doctors can usually start detecting a foetal heartbeat. Many women do not know they are pregnant at that point.

These state laws, if challenged, could come before the US Supreme Court's nine justices. Defenders of the right to abortion fear that the Court, which has become more conservative since Republican President Donald Trump appointed justices Neil Gorsuch and Brett Kavanaugh, could overturn or chip away at the 1973 ruling.

Glenn Herman is an obstetrician/gynaecologist (OB-GYN) who started practising medicine before Roe became law.

He later went on to sub-specialise in maternal and foetal medicine and has treated patients in Pennsylvania, New Jersey, Kentucky and Texas.

The recollections of specialists like Herman offer a view of life before Roe and a preview of what it could mean for women if the decision were overturned.

Medical practice before Roe

Dr Herman's pre-Roe experiences with abortion came not long after he graduated from New York Medical College in 1971. He moved to Philadelphia in 1972 for a three-year OB/GYN residency at Temple University. Learning the basics of his profession kept him "busy as never before, but one aspect of gynaecology was always there," he said.

"About three times a day, no matter what else I was doing, I would be called to the emergency room to take care of a miscarriage, or in medical terms, a 'spontaneous incomplete abortion.' I typically found a young woman bleeding heavily, in significant pain and looking quite scared," he said.

"We controlled the pain, bleeding and infection risk by doing a D&C [dilation & curettage]. Taking care of these women was an important medical activity, but it happened randomly over the course of a day. The issue was always there. It eventually became just a bit old, but it was always a part of the job."

About once a month, Herman said he encountered a 'septic abortion' – a potentially lethal infection in the uterus of a pregnant woman that he said was almost always the result of an illegal attempt at an abortion.

"These patients were filled up with antibiotics immediately, then taken to the operating room for a D&C. The infection made it very easy to tear a hole in the uterus. Days in the hospital were required for further administration of IV [intravenous] antibiotics. Some of these patients did die of infection and haemorrhage," he said.

Medical practice after Roe

In 1973, Roe became law, legalising abortion nationwide. "The dramatic decrease in septic abortions was obvious as soon as the law changed," Herman said.

He discovered fellow residents had also noticed a steep drop in spontaneous incomplete abortions – from about three patients a day to about two a week for every resident.

"I realized that about 75 per cent of our 'spontaneous incomplete abortions' had been far from 'spontaneous,'" Herman said.

Talking to patients, he learned more about how illegal abortions were being performed in the community. A medically untrained person was 'putting knitting needles through the cervix to rupture the foetal membrane.' They then told the women to go to the hospital when cramping and bleeding started.

He realised that the number of instrumented cases was beyond anything they had imagined: more than 70 times a month, residents had been 'completing abortions done by untrained but experienced abortionists.'

Herman noted that the amateurs were 'pretty good at it' because only about one patient a month turned septic. Of those, roughly one patient died each year.

"We never knew the extent of the problem until the problem went away," he said.

If Roe were overturned

Herman said that for economically disadvantaged women, outlawing abortion would mean that "knitting needles would reappear, and we would go back to what we saw before Roe."

Nowadays, since many more physicians have been trained to do abortions, wealthier patients could find ways to get 'expensive, surreptitious' illegal abortions, he said. Or wealthier women could afford to travel to countries where abortion remained legal.

"Of course, some women would not seek out these procedures, and some unwanted pregnancies would now be carried to term," he said.

Abortion as political football

Herman, still licensed to practise as an OB-GYN, said Roe "provided a solution to women who have an unwanted pregnancy". They ranged from "mothers who couldn't afford or care for another child to naive teenagers who couldn't even imagine being pregnant," he said. A major factor in unwanted pregnancies is contraceptive failure, he added.

After the Roe ruling, chronically ill patients were no longer forced to accept the risk of pregnancy. "Down Syndrome could now be approached, and foetal birth defects could be evaluated in terms of all available therapies," Herman said. "Family or personal histories suggesting the risk of genetic disease were no longer a bar to pregnancy."

Herman opposes women losing their legal right to abortion but recognises the issue has become deeply political.

When abortion was legalized in 1973, "at first it did not cause a whole lot of debate," he said. "When it came to be a very effective political 'wedge issue,' the uproar began."

27 June 2019

Abortion rate hits record high of 200,000 as mothers and older women fuel rise

By Gabriella Swerling, Social and Religious Affairs Editor

Abortions have reached the highest level ever in the UK, as new data reveals that 200,000 women had their pregnancies terminated last year.

The Department of Health and Social Care (DHSC) published figures today revealing that there were 200,608 abortions for women in England and Wales in 2018. This marked an increase of 4% or 192,900 from the previous year. A further 4,687 abortions were carried out on non-residents in 2018.

Experts said that the increase was as a result of older women and mothers being more likely to have abortions.

Clare Murphy, director of external affairs at abortion provider the British Pregnancy Advisory Service, said: "The reasons for the increase in abortions for older women in England and Wales are complex.

She said greater access to services was also needed for women who are already mothers.

"Unplanned pregnancy in the year after birth is not uncommon, particularly among women who are breastfeeding," she said.

"However, it is also possible that over the longer term couples are making different decisions about family size and the number of children they can afford and feel able to properly care for.

"The two-child benefit cap was designed to influence reproductive decision-making and we are certainly aware of cases where that has been a factor in a woman's decision to end a third, unplanned pregnancy."

Abortion rates by age range across England and Wales

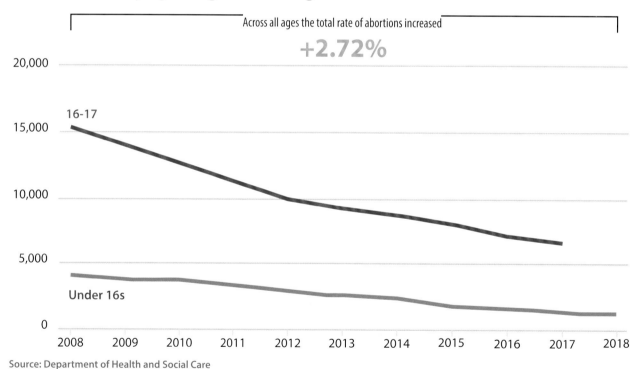

Across all ages the total rate of abortions increased

+2.72%

Source: Department of Health and Social Care

"Accessible contraceptive services are often focused on the needs of younger women and women over the age of 25 can in particular find themselves excluded from schemes providing free, pharmacy access to emergency contraception.

"As so many women in the UK rely on pills and condoms as their main methods of contraception, it is vital that there is swift access to emergency options when those methods fail or a pill is missed."

However, anti-abortion activists said that the latest abortion data represented a "national tragedy".

Clare McCarthy, spokeswoman for the Right to Life charity, said: "Every one of these abortions represents a failure of our society to protect the lives of babies in the womb and a failure to offer full support to women with unplanned pregnancies.

Abortion rate per 1,000 women by age, England and Wales

■ 2008 ▫ 2018

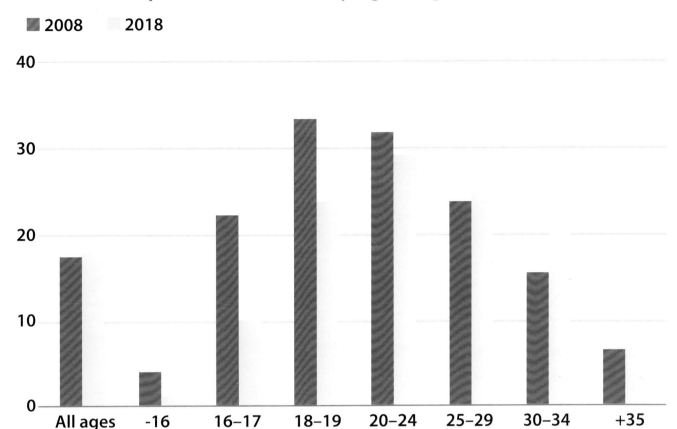

Source: Department of Health and Social Care

"Proposals from abortion campaigners to remove legal restrictions around abortion and introduce abortion right to birth would likely see these numbers get even worse."

There has been a sharp rise over the last decade in the proportion of abortions to women who are already mothers.

In 2018, 56% of abortions (111,633) were to women who had had one or more previous pregnancies that resulted in a live or stillbirth, up 5% on the 106,550 the previous year.

Less than half (48%) of abortions in 2008 were to women who had already had one or more previous births. Overall abortion rates have increased in the last decade for all women over the age of 25. The rates for women aged 30 to 34 increased from 15.6 per 1,000 women in 2008 to 19.9 in 2018.

Among those aged 35 and over, they have risen from 6.7 per 1,000 women in 2008 to 9.2 per 1,000 women in 2018.

In total, 34,380 women aged 35 and over had an abortion in 2018, up 6% on the 32,330 the year before. The data also showed there were 1,267 abortions to girls aged under 16 (0.6% of the total) in 2018.

Of these, 363 were to girls aged under 15 (0.2% of the total). Overall, the abortion rate among under-18s has been falling for a decade.

Nola Leach, chief executive at Christian Action Research and Education (CARE), added: "The fact that the abortion rate for women 35 or over has increased again since last year raises big questions about the pressures of modern life.

"The instability of cohabitation and the intense pressure for couples to maintain two incomes are taking a heavy price.

"It's time we ended the culture where abortion is seen as the only option. Women need to be supported and informed about the wide variety of alternatives out there."

A Department of Health and Social Care spokesperson said: "We are committed to maintaining a safe and caring environment for all women who need an abortion. It is encouraging to see that the number of women under 18 having abortions has fallen – however, we do want to better understand why rates in other age groups are increasing and we are monitoring this trend closely. We are looking at ways to increase access to contraception, which will be set out in PHE's reproductive health action plan to be published this year."

13 June 2019

Abortions rise worldwide when US cuts funding to women's health clinics, study finds

An article from The Conversation.

THE CONVERSATION

By Yana Rodgers, Professor of Labor Studies, Rutgers University

Advancing Republican efforts to reduce access to abortion, Secretary of State Mike Pompeo announced on 26 March that the Trump administration will further restrict federal funding to health providers abroad that perform, promote or even talk about abortions.

The move expands the 'global gag rule' Trump imposed in 2017. It substantially expands the number of groups affected by cutting funding to any organisation with a foreign partner that provides abortions – even if those overseas groups are not, themselves, US government-funded.

First implemented under Ronald Reagan in 1984, the global gag rule has been rescinded by every Democrat and reinstated by every Republican to occupy the Oval Office, reflecting the partisan nature of abortion.

Supporters of the global gag rule say defunding abortion providers will reduce abortions.

However, researchers from Stanford University in 2011 found that this US policy actually made women in sub-Saharan Africa twice as likely to have an abortion.

Gag rule increases abortions in Latin America and Africa

My recent study, published in November 2018, confirms those findings in Africa and shows that the global gag rule had an even greater effect in Latin America.

Analysing abortion data from 51 developing countries between 2001 and 2008 – which encompassed the reproductive decisions of about 6.3 million women – I found that women in Latin America were three times more likely to have an abortion while the global gag rule was in effect.

Reflecting this impact, the percentage of pregnancies in Latin America that ended in abortion rose from 23 per cent

Abortion around the world

Unsafe abortions are a major problem in parts of the developing world, according to a worldwide tally taken between 2010 and 2014. In Latin America, 75 percent of abortions are performed illegally.

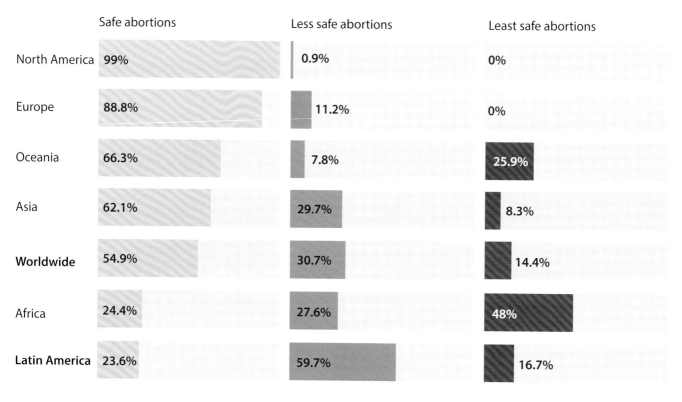

	Safe abortions	Less safe abortions	Least safe abortions
North America	99%	0.9%	0%
Europe	88.8%	11.2%	0%
Oceania	66.3%	7.8%	25.9%
Asia	62.1%	29.7%	8.3%
Worldwide	54.9%	30.7%	14.4%
Africa	24.4%	27.6%	48%
Latin America	23.6%	59.7%	16.7%

Chart: The Conversation, CC-BY-ND Source: The Lancet

in 1994, under the Clinton administration, to 32 per cent by 2010, after two terms of the Bush administration.

In the United States, where abortion is legal nationwide, about 18 to 23 per cent of pregnancies end in abortion.

How a US law hurts women abroad

Funding cuts under the global gag rule cause healthcare staff reductions, clinic closures and contraceptive shortages. Without family planning counselling and birth control, there are more unintended pregnancies – and, consequently, more abortions.

Numerous studies confirm that making abortions harder to get doesn't stop them from happening. It just makes them less safe, because the procedure is not necessarily performed in sterile facilities by qualified doctors.

Latin America, a heavily Catholic region, has the world's most restrictive abortion laws.

Six countries, including Honduras, Nicaragua and El Salvador, completely ban abortion.

Others permit it only in extreme cases like rape, incest or maternal health.

Latin America also has the world's highest rate of illicit abortions, according to a 2017 study in *The Lancet*. 75 per cent of all abortions in Latin America are performed illegally.

Since Trump reinstated the global gag rule in 2017, health workers in developing countries have reported drastic reductions in the availability of contraception, teen sex education and family planning services.

27 March 2019

When religious ideology drives abortion policy, poor women suffer the consequences

An article from The Conversation.

THE CONVERSATION

By Gretchen E. Ely, Professor and Associate Dean for Academic Affairs, University at Buffalo, The State University of New York

In Northern Ireland, Catholics and Protestants are frequently segregated, with some neighborhoods divided by barbed wire fences, reflecting deep historical conflicts between the faiths.

90% of Northern Ireland's 1.87 million people are Christian, with Protestants, once the solid majority there, now slightly outnumbering Catholics. But members of these faiths remain divided decades after a 1997 peace agreement meant to end sectarian violence in the region.

Northern Irish politicians do agree on one thing lately, *The New York Times* reports: banning abortion.

It is illegal in Northern Ireland to end a pregnancy unless it endangers the mother's life, though 65% of Northern Ireland's population supports abortion. As a result, women who seek abortions typically go to England, where abortion is legal.

But, as my research on cases of low-income abortion patients shows, not everyone can afford abortion expenses. That includes women in the United States, where restrictive abortion laws mean the nearest clinic may be many miles away.

Unaffordable abortion

In one 2017 study, I examined data of over 2,300 patients in Ireland, Northern Ireland and the Isle of Man who had received financial assistance from abortion funds, charitable organisations that help people access abortions they can't afford.

Though the Republic of Ireland legalised abortion in May 2018, leaving Northern Ireland as the only nation on the British Isles with an abortion ban, our research took place when abortion was illegal in both nations.

The average abortion expense for our sample was US$585, while patients had on average just $307 at their disposal to pay for the procedure. 84% of these abortion-seekers were single, 34% were age 21 or under and 8% were minors. They had, on average, two children each.

This profile is comparable to that of the almost 4,000 abortion fund service recipients in the United States whose data we also studied. In the US, abortion is legal nationally but highly restricted in some states.

We found many similarities between the patients. The American patients had, on average, $422 to contribute to abortions that cost around $1775. They were also young, single parents of two. These American low-income abortion-seekers travelled, on average, 140 miles for their procedure.

Penalizing the poor

Recent changes to US family planning policy highlight another parallel between Northern Ireland and the United States: the influence of religion in reproductive health policy.

In mid-August, Planned Parenthood announced its withdrawal from Title X – a Nixon-era family planning programme for low-income patients – due to a new requirement that Title X medical providers cannot also offer abortions.

Religion in health policy

Many nations in Europe can be classified as predominantly Christian, much like the American South and Northern Ireland. But few allow religious ideology to influence their reproductive health laws.

In France, 60% of people identify as Christian, abortion is legal, and 80% of the French support the procedure in all or most circumstances, according to the Pew Research Center.

Legal abortion is similarly acceptable throughout Western Europe, Pew polling finds, with public support at 60% in Portugal, 65% in Italy and 72% in Spain – all majority Catholic nations.

Catholic Ireland, where even condoms used to be banned, recently voted to legalise abortion in the first trimester. The momentous decision was spurred by the death of a 31-year-old woman who was denied an abortion after miscarriage.

Title X funds have never been used to pay for abortion services. But by eliminating funding for facilities that offer abortions in addition to other reproductive services, the Trump administration rule may leave millions of low-income Planned Parenthood patients without family planning care.

The new rule is part of an old American effort, promoted by Christian activists and lawmakers, to make legal abortions as difficult as possible to obtain.

The new Title X rule builds on the 1976 Hyde Amendment, which prevents federal dollars from paying for abortion expenses. Low-income women relying on programmes like Medicaid for health insurance must pay out-of-pocket for abortion, reallocating money that would otherwise go to food and rent.

While most manage to access a wanted abortion, research shows, some poor American women end up carrying unwanted pregnancies to term against their will.

Many states in the southern US – a conservative region where 76% of residents identify as Christian – require a waiting period of up to three days for patients to 'reflect' on abortion decisions. In practice, that means two mandatory in-person trips to the clinic and higher medical costs.

In Tennessee, where there is a 48-hour abortion waiting period, my recent research found that abortion-seekers from the mountainous Appalachian region reported financial and personal strain, as well as problems arranging child care and transportation. Appalachia is a rural, remote region where healthcare access is already compromised. The 48-hour waiting period likely puts legal abortion out of reach for some.

Evidence-based policies

Irish voters' willingness to modernise abortion laws against Catholic teaching reflects a reality that my research lays bare: reproductive health policies based on ideology rather than scientific evidence fail to serve the public.

Studies show that abortion rates across countries are similar regardless of legality. So making abortions illegal or inaccessible generally does not stop women from getting them.

Wealthier abortion patients with adequate resources will overcome costs and other barriers that restrictive abortions law throw in front of them. Poor abortion-seekers are more likely to seek unsafe, even deadly, procedures.

Research from Latin America confirms this. This socially conservative, heavily Catholic region has the world's most restrictive abortion laws. It also has the highest rates of clandestine abortions.

Religious freedom is critical in any free society, and faith provides a vital source of comfort for many people. But evidence shows that religion can be a burden, not a blessing, when it comes to reproductive health.

30 August 2019

A new poll shows what really interests 'pro-lifers': controlling women

According to their own survey responses, anti-abortion voters are hostile to gender equality in practically every aspect.

By Jill Filipovic

According to self-identified 'pro-life' advocates, the fundamental divide between those who want to outlaw abortion and those who want to keep it legal comes down to one question: when does life begin? Anti-abortion advocacy pushes the view that life begins at conception; the name of their movement carefully centres the conceit that opposition to abortion rights is simply about wanting to save human lives.

A new poll shows that's a lie. The 'pro-life' movement is fundamentally about misogyny.

A Supermajority/PerryUndem survey released this week divides respondents by their position on abortion, and then tracks their answers to 10 questions on gender equality more generally. On every question, anti-abortion voters were significantly more hostile to gender equity than pro-choice voters.

Do men make better political leaders than women? More than half of anti-abortion voters agreed. Do you want there to be equal numbers of men and women in positions of power in America? Fewer than half of abortion opponents said yes – compared with 80% of pro-choicers, who said they want women to share in power equally.

> *"They don't believe sexism is a problem, and they're hostile to women's rights. Pro-lifers are sexists in denial – yes, the women too."*

Anti-abortion voters don't like the #MeToo movement. They don't think the lack of women in positions of power impacts women's equality. They don't think access to birth control impacts women's equality. They don't think the way women are treated in society is an important issue in the 2020 election.

In other words, they don't believe sexism is a problem, and they're hostile to women's rights. Pro-lifers are sexists in denial – yes, the women too.

In the aftermath of the 2016 election, mostly white pundits wondered if Donald Trump's white male base was motivated by 'economic anxiety'. We heard this over and over: Trump voters aren't the racist deplorables the liberal media (of which those same pundits were a part) makes them out to be. They're decent people who have been hurt by free trade agreements, increasing Chinese economic dominance, the decimation of unions, a thinning social safety net and stagnating wages. (Why those same people would then turn around and vote for a party that kills unions, tears up the safety net and blocks minimum wage raises while cutting taxes for CEOs went unexplained.)

Then came the social scientists – and whaddaya know? Trump voters weren't motivated by economic anxiety as much as fear of 'cultural displacement'. White Christian men (and many of their wives) were so used to their cultural, political and economic dominance that they perceived the ascension of other groups as a threat.

To put it in more straightforward terms, they were racist (and sexist), and saw in Trump a kindred spirit who would work for their interests – their primary interest being a symbolic reassertion of their cultural dominance. Trump's continued appeals to his racist base, coupled with his efforts to help the rich and screw the working class, have only confirmed this conclusion: his base still cheers him on, economic anxiety be damned.

The American anti-abortion movement invented this kind of political gaslighting. The Catholic church, an unabashedly misogynist institution that to this day refuses to allow women into positions of power, had long opposed abortion (but not for all that long – until about 150 years ago, the Catholic view was that abortion was permissible through the first few months of pregnancy).

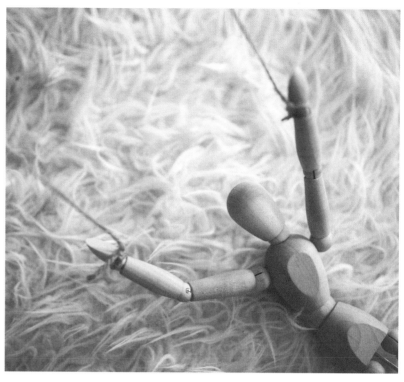

> *"The goal of abortion opponents is clear: they do not want women to be equal players in society."*

But evangelicals didn't seem to think much about abortion until an earlier pet issue, racial segregation, began to fall out of favour. Around the same time, women's social roles were rapidly changing. The birth control pill brought with it an avalanche of opportunities and freedoms, and women, finally fully able to have sex for fun and prevent pregnancy, took full advantage. The ability to delay a pregnancy – and later, the ability to legally end one – meant that women didn't have to choose between romance and ambition (and it meant women could be choosier about romance, making a more considered decision about who and whether to marry).

The goal of abortion opponents is clear: they do not want women to be equal players in society

This undermined the whole right-wing Christian project, which was, and remains, thoroughly invested in a nuclear family with a father at the head. And indeed, right-wing arguments against abortion used to invoke conservative gender tropes much more often – that abortion undermined the traditional family, for example.

Those arguments began to fall out of favour in a more feminist world, so the anti-abortion movement pivoted towards "life". It was convenient: erase the pregnant woman and focus on the foetus. Defending life, abortion opponents have long claimed, has absolutely nothing to do with opposing rights for women.

Except, of course, that it does. Abortion rights advocates have spent decades pointing out that these self-styled pro-lifers don't seem to care much about 'life' once a baby is born. They want to cut aid to needy children and healthcare to poor mothers and pregnant women. They oppose contraception and sex education – the most effective ways to reduce the abortion rate. Many of them continue to support a president who separates small children from their parents and keeps them in squalid cages. 'Life', it seems, has precious little to do with being 'pro-life'.

This survey is another example of how abortion opposition is tied up in a whole knot of misogyny.

Women, according to more than three-quarters of anti-abortion survey respondents, 'are too easily offended'. More than 70% of 'pro-lifers' in the survey agree that women interpret innocent remarks or acts as being sexist – women, in other words, are a touch hysterical and perhaps not to be trusted. While 82% of pro-choice respondents said that the country would be better off with more women in political office, just 34% of abortion opponents agreed.

It's not about 'life'. It's about the fact that abortion is inexorably tied to women's freedoms and female power. If women can't decide for themselves when and whether to have children – if having sex can mean being forced into motherhood – women also won't be able to decide our own futures. We know that being forced to continue a pregnancy makes women more likely to remain in poverty. It makes women more likely to remain in abusive relationships. It hurts their children. It makes women more likely to die.

If you don't want women to be equal, a great way to force that ideal is to strip women of our rights to our own bodies and reproductive decisions. And the goal of abortion opponents is clear: they do not want women to be equal players in society.

Thanks to the glut of data on what actually motivates Trump voters, you don't hear the 'economic anxiety' argument made much any more – it's usually referenced derisively. It's time to give the claim of being 'pro-life' the same treatment.

22 August 2019

The 'escorts' who ward off anti-abortion protesters at Mississippi's lone clinic

'Clinic escorts' create a buffer between protesters and women arriving at the clinic as its role becomes ever-more important.

By Khushbu Shah

Kim Gibson wore a pastel rainbow-striped vest with the words "clinic escort" in bold, black letters as she glanced over at the arriving white van. She was irritated by the sudden appearance in Jackson of more Christian anti-abortion protesters in front of Mississippi's lone abortion clinic.

She watched as the vehicle pulled up, letting out two sisters. They dropped picket signs onto the Jackson sidewalk before their mother drove off to park. When she walked back with her teenage son, Gibson yelled: "Shame what you do to these children. Shame, shame, shame."

The young boy held up a poster nearly as tall as himself, with a picture of an aborted foetus: 'The wages of sin is death,' it said.

Gibson marched down the parking lot to turn up the song on the speakers in front of the clinic doors and Gwen Stefani lets everyone know she ain't no hollaback girl for the seventh time that day.

It's part of the 'going in' soundtrack – all upbeat songs – for patients arriving at the clinic. Another escort dances along, facing the protesters, trying to create a buffer between the protesters and women going in for state-mandated counselling sessions or procedures.

Mississippi is the only state in the south with a lone abortion provider and attracts special attention from protesters. As a wave of states across the US, including conservative southern states like Mississippi, pass ever stricter anti-abortion laws, the role of such clinics has become ever more important.

Mississippi is one of nine states to pass restrictive abortion bans. These all come as a reinvigorated evangelical right in the US challenges access to abortion. The bans are designed to place pressure on Roe v. Wade, the landmark Supreme Court ruling that protected a pregnant woman's legal right to choose to have an abortion.

And in order to function, there is one group of people the clinics desperately need: the escorts who help patients run the gauntlet of protesters determined to stop them having abortions.

Here in this corner of Mississippi, they are the Pink House Defenders: nicknamed for the garish color of the Jackson Women's Health Organization's exterior walls.

All the escorts are volunteers. Most have full-time jobs and schedule work shifts around clinic days. They have been organised for more than six years by 60-year-old Derenda Hancock.

Gibson's and Hancock's attention shifts quickly to new protesters, particularly one clad in a pink vest, motioning for a car driving up to the abortion clinic to roll down the passenger window. At first, the passenger hesitates but when the teen tugs at her pink vest, suggesting she works at the clinic (she doesn't) the passenger rolls down the window.

A pamphlet is thrust into the car and the girl speaks to those inside: 'What did your baby do wrong?'

Frantically, Gibson motions to the car to keep driving. "C'mon, sweetie!" Hancock sighed, rolling her eyes. "This is Mississippi. They are too polite to drive past these people."

Dale, Gibson's husband is another escort. As a patient makes her way from the lot to the front entrance, protesters peek through the gap in the black tarp, pleading for the woman to reconsider. Using a tambourine, Dale tries to drown out the "sidewalk counseling", as protesters call their work. The song coming through the speakers is "Twist and Shout".

Each volunteer plays a role in keeping the chaos to a minimum, when they can.

James Parker, Hancock's long-time partner, keeps an eye on the traffic in and out of the parking lot. Another morning, before patients arrive, Parker repaints the white parking spot dividers to mitigate potential traffic jams. When he told colleagues at his power plant where he spent his off days, they assumed he was picketing the clinic.

"They only think it's admirable if you're protesting," he said.

Escorts would be unnecessary if not for the protesters who seem to match them shift-for-shift. A 73-year-old woman protester claims she was the first one to start protesting the Jackson abortion clinic more than seven years ago. Now, she tries to make sure at least one anti-abortion protester is covering the shift each morning.

"Good morning. How are you?" another protester asks Hancock later one morning, walking towards the tarp-covered pink wall begging a patient to reconsider. Hancock can't help but respond: "Better before you got here."

Spending so much time together, the escorts have gotten to know the protesters and which ones to worry about.

One morning, Hancock and Gibson lean into their portable red chairs at the entrance of the lot, not worried about the trio in front of them. The 73-year-old protester can't scream

very loudly, Hancock says. "[Her friend] is loud, though," Gibson offers. Hancock points to a younger woman and labels her a "screecher". This mother, who has brought four of her children to protest, Hancock relays, has 10 children but they're quieter than their cousins, 14 in total.

"They're good kids," she added.

Right now, the larger set is on a road trip with their parents. Hancock doesn't hold it against the children. She even gave the kids a list of sights to see as they make their way around the midwest and keeps tabs on them through their father's Facebook page.

With the recent attention on anti-abortion Bills in the south, anti-abortion protesters and women seeking abortions aren't the only ones showing up. In recent days, an older man from California joined the tight-knit group, claiming he's a pro-choice lay minister. He himself would like to offer counseling options to women after they've had an abortion, he tells the group.

Frustrated by his presence, Hancock refuses. There's already enough religion being thrown around healthcare here, she points out.

"It's just so much. Everywhere. All the time," Gibson said.

13 August 2019

I was an anti-abortion teenager ready to protest outside clinics – but then something huge changed my mind

Now Ealing Council's safe zone has been ruled legal, it brings me relief that people like my misguided 17-year-old self won't be able to do what I nearly did. But we need to go further.

By Olivia Campbell

I was 17 when I was asked to protest outside an abortion clinic.

A friend who I attended the same all-girls Catholic convent school with wanted me to come with her to the Marie Stopes clinic in Ealing. As a way of protest, we were to stand holding hands, silently praying for all the innocent souls who'd never be born while hopefully persuading women to not commit such a 'sin'. We were to be led by a boy who attended a certain all-boys school in West Brompton.

I regretfully admit that at this age I agreed with ideas that most definitely aligned with pro-life rhetoric. A combination of subtle religious teachings and the knowledge from hours researching an essay on the ethics of abortion, I couldn't understand how anybody would want to harm the life inside of them. I fully recognise that these views are abhorrent now, but at the time, I fully believed that women should be forced to carry pregnancies to term.

Yet, despite being armed with this self-righteous thinking, something inside of me was torn. I had been so sure of my moral standing before but when it was time to protest, said action felt extremely wrong. One question kept popping up: who was I, someone who'd never faced such a decision, to judge those probably undergoing one of the most traumatic events in their lives? No woman casually decides to pop along to the abortion clinic, ready to excavate their uterus and move on with their day.

Catholicism teaches to not judge the actions of others, but here I was, deciding whether to condemn, albeit silently, people I'd never met.

After much soul-searching, I realised how detrimental these views were. I recognised how harmful my actions had the potential to be, all because I felt my 'opinion' should be a reason to take away a woman's bodily autonomy.

In that moment I decided that I would not be attending a protest led by someone who would never have to decide whether to carry a foetus to term. I have been unapologetically pro-choice ever since.

It brought me great pleasure to hear that Ealing Council were going to be implementing a 330ft buffer zone outside the same clinic I had been asked to protest at five years before. The 2018 decision came into existence after reports found that women were suffering 'intimidation, harassment and distress' at the hands of protesters. The Public Spaces Protection Order (PSPO) prevents sanctimonious individuals from carrying out actions such as waving around placards of dead foetuses and harassing women acquiring care.

Last week, the Court of Appeal ruled that the safe zone was legal. Despite anti-abortion groups claiming the buffer infringed on their right to free speech and religion, Ealing Council will be allowed to carry on implementing it.

This religious passive aggression that is being cracked down on is just as harmful as it would be if verbal abuse and violence was a factor. Women have long spoken of the distress they felt seeing anti-abortion groups outside the clinic, with some even speaking of the long-lasting damage such an encounter can have.

In 2018, more than 200,000 abortion procedures took place. The medical procedure isn't going away anytime soon, and unfortunately, neither are the people who protest. Anti-abortion groups claim that women getting procedures do not have a right to privacy, making them believe their vilification of women about to undergo a potentially traumatic procedure is justified.

People have the right to freedom of religion, but this does not mean that they get to harass and intimidate those receiving treatment. This should be common sense but here we are having to use protection orders on medical facilities.

I am so grateful that people with these intentions will not be able to target individuals. It brings me relief that people like my misguided 17-year-old self won't be able to do what I nearly did. I can't even begin to imagine the emotional damage my decision to silently protest could have inflicted on such vulnerable individuals.

However, this is not enough. The buffer zone will only last another two years before it runs out and the whole process of implementing it starts again. Furthermore, these zones are not mandatory across the UK and there is currently no government legislation in place, meaning that buffers are at the prerogative of already-burdened councils.

The assault on bodily autonomy is happening all across the planet. However, there are parts of the world were laws and legislature do try to protect women. In parts of Canada and Australia zones from 10 to 150 metres in size have been lawfully implemented, prohibiting certain destructive behaviours.

The UK Government needs to follow this example and move forward with legislature to implement these zones in any of the abortion clinics across the country. Not only to ensure the emotional wellbeing of patients, but to prevent harassment and intimidation.

It's been six years since I was asked to protest outside Marie Stopes. It's been six years since I decided that I was pro-choice and would vehemently defend a women's right to their own body. No woman should have to suffer because other people decide it's their business to try and control them.

28 August 2019

This is why it matters the BBC didn't include abortion information after its *Call the Midwife* episode

The BBC views abortion as too 'contentious' to mention – our society clearly thinks otherwise.

By Katherine O'Brien, Head of Media and Policy Research at Bpas

Last week, 8.9 million of us watched the harrowing story of a young mother who lost her life due to complications from a backstreet abortion in Sunday's episode of *Call the Midwife*. It was heartbreaking viewing, and was also a poignant reminder of just how grateful we all should be to the campaigners in the 1960s who fought for the rights that are easily taken for granted today.

> *"There were links for those affected by miscarriage, stillbirth, addiction and gender dysphoria (among other issues.) But the 'information and support' for those affected by abortion did not exist."*

After the programme, the BBC advertised the availability of their Action Line website for viewers seeking 'information and support for issues covered in the programme. Yet for those seeking advice on *Call the Midwife's* central storyline, there was none. There were links for those affected by

miscarriage, stillbirth, addiction and gender dysphoria (among other issues.) But the 'information and support' for those affected by abortion did not exist.

'Contentious'

Women contacted the charity I work for, the British Pregnancy Advisory Service, to raise this omission, and we got in touch with the BBC assuming this was simply an error. However, in response, the BBC stated that they had made an active decision to exclude information on abortion – because this aspect of healthcare, which has been legal in certain circumstances for over 50 years, is too 'contentious'. The BBC reply said:

"It isn't possible for the BBC Action Line to offer support for abortion and similarly contentious issues without referring people either to campaigning organisations which take a particular stance on an issue or to organisations which provide it.

"Doing so could imply the BBC supported one side or another in any contentious issue which it does not do in its coverage."

We were completely shocked

We were completely shocked by this response. Far from being impartial, the BBC are in fact 'supporting a side' through a policy which treats abortion as different to all other the medical procedures and conditions they choose to include on the site.

In this country, abortion is a routine, overwhelmingly accepted aspect of women's healthcare. One in three women will have an abortion in their lifetime, and it is the most common gynaecological procedure in the country. The vast majority of the public support a woman's right to choose, including those with religious beliefs. Indeed support for abortion among Catholics has doubled in the past 20 years. MPs from across both sides of the House have voted repeatedly in favour of liberalising our abortion law and ending the shameful denial of reproductive choice for women resident in Northern Ireland.

The BBC views abortion as too 'contentious' to mention – our society clearly thinks otherwise.

Leave silence stigma back in the 1960s

That's why today, Bpas has joined together with medical Royal Colleges and other women's healthcare bodies to call on the BBC to reverse this shameful position. To exclude information about abortion from their website stigmatises the doctors, nurses and midwives who work tirelessly in our clinics, and it also stigmatises the women they care for.

As last week's episode of *Call the Midwife* so powerfully articulated, women bear a huge cost when they cannot access safe, legal abortion services and advice. The young mother who had the backstreet abortion used £7 from her family's savings kitty to fund the procedure, but ultimately paid with her life.

So in 2019, we shouldn't view abortion care as "contentious" – we should celebrate it.

Celebrate the fact that it not only protects women's health but also enables women to have control of their fertility, their bodies and, ultimately, the course of their lives. Which is why we urge the BBC to bring their policy on abortion into the twenty-first century – and leave the stigma and silence back in the 1960s.

A BBC spokesperson said:

"Abortion is a controversial subject across the UK, but there's no reason why the BBC cannot link to advice sites which provide information on it. BBC Action line advice around Call The Midwife links to a number of sources of pregnancy advice and information, including the NHS website which includes information about abortion."

14 February 2019

Key Facts

- One in three women will have an abortion in their lifetime. (page 1)

- Most abortions in England, Wales and Scotland are carried out before 24 weeks of pregnancy. (page 1)

- In 1967, Parliament passed the Abortion Act, later amended by the Human Fertilisation and Embryology Act 1990. (page 3)

- Health professionals are not required to perform or participate in an abortion if they have a moral or conscientious objection. They still have a duty to participate in an abortion, if it is necessary to save the life of a woman or to prevent serious injury. (page 3)

- Over the last 10 years, abortion rates have decreased year on year for women aged under 18. Abortion rates have been increasing for women aged over 35. (page 4)

- Unlike any other medical procedure and for no clinical reason whatsoever 2 doctors must authorise every request for an abortion. (page 12)

- Abortion is one of the most common medical procedures globally. (page 13)

- Abortion is freely available to women in 67 countries, with another 56 countries allowing it on health grounds. Abortion is banned outright in 26 countries, according to the Center for Reproductive Rights. (page 13)

- Most opposition to abortion rights stems from religious beliefs. (page 13)

- In 1973, an important US Supreme Court decision called Roe v. Wade established a woman's right to abortion, based on her right to privacy. (page 14)

- As of 1 January 2019, the law allowing access to abortion in the Republic of Ireland is the Health (Regulation of Termination of Pregnancy) Act 2018. This legislation followed from the 66.4% Yes vote in the referendum to repeal the Eighth Amendment in May 2018. (page 18)

- The Abortion Act introduced in the rest of the UK in 1967 was never extended to Northern Ireland, which has meant that every year hundreds of women have had to travel to England for terminations. They even had to pay for them until Westminster changed the law in 2018 to cover the cost. (page 19)

- In July 2019, Westminster passed legislation which said that if the Northern Irish Assembly had not been re-established by 21 October then the law in Northern Ireland would be changed... That means that a new legal framework for abortion law must be in place by 31 March 2020. (page 20)

- More than 200,000 UK women received an abortion in 2018, setting an all-time high rate of abortion in England and Wales. (page 23)

- The natural gender ratio for humans is 100 female babies to 105 male babies. (page 24)

- The sex ratio in China was worst in 2005 where approximately 100 female babies were born in comparison to 118 male births. (page 24)

- India outlawed the selective abortion of female foetuses in 1994 but the practice remains commonplace in the country, where parents often see boys as breadwinners and girls as costly liabilities. (page 25)

- In May, Alabama lawmakers voted to ban abortions in nearly all cases. Georgia, Kentucky, Louisiana, Missouri, Mississippi and Ohio have approved 'heartbeat bills' that effectively prohibit abortions after six to eight weeks of pregnancy, when doctors can usually start detecting a foetal heartbeat. Many women do not know they are pregnant at that point. (page 26)

- The Department of Health and Social Care (DHSC) published figures today revealing that there were 200,608 abortions for women in England and Wales in 2018. This marked an increase of 4% or 192,900 from the previous year. (page 28)

- Latin America has the world's highest rate of illicit abortions, according to a 2017 study in *The Lancet*. 75% of all abortions in Latin America are performed illegally. (page 31)

Abortion

A procedure which prematurely ends a pregnancy through the death and expulsion of the foetus. It can occur naturally (spontaneous abortion), but this is more commonly referred to as a miscarriage. The term 'abortion' usually refers to the deliberate termination of an unwanted pregnancy (induced abortion).

The Abortion Act 1967

This Act decriminalised abortion in cases where it had been certified by two doctors that certain grounds had been met, such as a serious risk to the mental or physical health of the pregnant woman.

Ciocia Basia

A Berlin-based activist group helping to organise safe abortions for women from countries where it is illegal.

Conception

The act of fertilisation, where an egg (ovum) joins together with a sperm (spermatozoon) to form an embryo or zygote. This term describes the moment a woman becomes pregnant.

Contraception

Anything which prevents conception, or pregnancy, from taking place. 'Barrier methods', such as condoms, work by stopping sperm from reaching an egg during intercourse and are also effective in preventing sexually transmitted infections (STI's). Hormonal methods such as the contraceptive pill change the way a woman's body works to prevent an egg from being fertilised. Emergency contraception, commonly known as the 'morning-after pill', is used after unprotected sex to prevent a fertilised egg from becoming implanted in the womb.

Embryo (zygote)

Between day 14 and week eight of pregnancy, the fertilised egg is referred to as an embryo. A zygote is simply the scientific term for the fertilised egg which is made by the joining of an egg (ovum) and sperm (spermatozoon). After the eighth week of pregnancy an unborn baby is referred to as a foetus.

Female infanticide

Infanticide is the unlawful killing of very young children and babies. Female infanticide specifically refers to the practice of killing female babies and young girls and is a practice that has been reported in India, China and parts of Africa, Asia and the Middle East.

Foetus

The unborn offspring of an animal or human being that has developed from an embryo.

Gestation

The development period of an embryo or foetus between conception and birth. As the exact date of conception in humans can be difficult to identify it is usually dated from the beginning of a woman's previous menstrual period.

Neonatal

Referring to an unborn child, or the period of time before a child is born.

Obstetricians and gynaecologists

An obstetrician or gynaecologist is a person who specialises in treating diseases of the female reproductive organs.

Pro-choice

Pro-choice supporters believe that it is a woman's right to choose whether or not to continue with a pregnancy. They also believe that the choice to have an abortion should be available to all.

Pro-life

Pro-life supporters believe that life begins at the moment of conception and think that an unborn child, foetus or embryo has the same rights as any other living person. They believe that the law should be changed so that abortion would be heavily restricted or outlawed in the UK.

Roe v. Wade

Roe v. Wade was a 1973 landmark decision by the US Supreme Court. The court ruled that a state law that banned abortions (except to save the life of the mother) was unconstitutional, effectively legalising the procedure across the United States.

Sex-selective abortion

The practice of terminating a pregnancy based upon the anticipated sex of the child (most often a girl).

Terminate

A term meaning 'to bring something to an end', an abortion is sometimes referred to as a termination.

Activities

Brainstorming

- In small groups, discuss what you know about abortion and why it is such a controversial topic.

- What is the current UK legislation on abortion?

- What are some of the reasons a woman might decide to have an abortion?

- Why is abortion often considered medically necessary?

- Why do some people oppose a woman's right to have an abortion?

- What effects can laws restricting abortion have on women's health and on wider society?

Research

- Look at the 2018 abortion statistics for England and Wales (page 4). Research abortion statistics in another European country and see how they compare to the UK. Make some notes about your findings then share with the rest of your class. Discuss possible reasons for the differences or similarities between the statistics.

- Research attitudes to abortion in the US. Have any laws changed in recent years? What factors do you think might influence a change in abortion legislation? Write a short summary and then feedback to your class.

- Conduct an anonymous poll to find out whether people in your year group believe that abortion should be legal or illegal. When you have gathered your results, create a graph or pie chart to demonstrate the different percentages.

- Conduct some online research into different religious groups and how their views on abortion vary. Which religions are largely supportive of legalised abortion and which are strictly opposed to it in all circumstances?

Design

- Create a leaflet for young women who are considering an abortion. It should give advice about where they can go, who they can talk to, the risks, the alternatives and the practicalities.

- Choose one of the articles from this book and create an illustration that highlights the key themes of the piece.

- Design a series of social media posts or a campaign that could be used by a pro-choice charity to spread their message and promote alternatives to abortion.

Oral

- In small groups, debate whether you think men should be given a say in whether women have abortions.

- Stage a debate in which half of your class argues on the side of the pro-life argument and the other argues for pro-choice. Think carefully about the views of your allocated side and try to understand why they believe what they do.

- Consider the articles on pages 24 and 25. As a class, discuss the reasons for, and the impact of, sex-selective abortions.

- Religious beliefs aside, in small groups, consider other possible reasons for holding an anti-abortion stance. What are they? Discuss with the rest of the class.

Reading/writing

- Read the article *Here's what legalising abortion has meant for US women* on page 26 and answer the following questions:

  - What was Roe v. Wade?

  - Why does Dr Herman oppose the overturning of Roe v. Wade?

  - Do you believe there should be limits on a woman's right to abortion?

- Write an article which will explore the following question: 'Why is it important to educate students about contraception, pregnancy and abortion?'

- Write a blog post exposing the truth about abortion law in Ireland. Use the articles in this book to help you.

- Read the article *Abortion rate hits record high of 200,000 as mothers and older women fuel rise* on page 28. What are the reasons given to explain the contrast in abortion rates between older women and females under the age of 25? Write a short paragraph summarising your findings.

U
unsafe abortion   15–17, 26–7
uterine perforation   16

W
World Health Organisation (WHO), on unsafe
   abortions   15–17

Acknowledgements

The publisher is grateful for permission to reproduce the material in this book. While every care has been taken to trace and acknowledge copyright, the publisher tenders its apology for any accidental infringement or where copyright has proved untraceable. The publisher would be pleased to come to a suitable arrangement in any such case with the rightful owner.

Images

Cover image courtesy of iStock. All other images courtesy of Freepik, Pixabay and Unsplash.

Illustrations

Don Hatcher: pages 12 & 27. Simon Kneebone: pages 9 & 24. Angelo Madrid: pages 7 & 15.

Additional acknowledgements

With thanks to the Independence team: Shelley Baldry, Danielle Lobban, Jackie Staines and Jan Sunderland.

Tracy Biram

Cambridge, January 2020